1

Reflections of an American in Japan

Anne Crescini

Driving Me Crazy About It

ISBN-13: 978-1481147729

ISBN-10: 1481147722

Cover Design: Jim Xavier

Back Cover Author Image: Riz Crescini

For the Japanese people

Table of Contents

Part I. Five Things I Love

Part II. Five Things I Don't Get

Important Japanese terms used in this book:

onsen-hot spring

ofuro-Japanese-style bathtub

bento-boxed lunch

gaman-endurance; perseverance

meiwaku-bother or trouble

tanshin funin-to live apart from family for work

gaijin-foreigner

okaeshi-return gift

omiyage-souvenir

boshi techo-maternal and child health handbook

uchi-your inner circle, including family and close friends

soto-everyone not in your inner circle

jukensei-student studying for high school or university entrance exams

oppai-breasts, breast milk, or breastfeeding

Introduction

I have wanted to write about my love-hate relationship with Japan for years, but have always been too busy: work, family responsibilities, travel. One day I was reading a book by one of my favorite authors, Mark Batterson, and he was talking about having the same feelings before he wrote his first book. He had been felt called to write a book for years, but something always kept him from doing it. He felt overwhelmed by the idea. He didn't know where to start. He didn't have confidence. Why would anyone want to read what he had to say anyway? If you think about it, all writers have to have a kind of pride, or else, why do they think people would take time out of their busy schedules to read what they have to say?

Batterson said one day he just decided to do it. He did not know how he would get it published, or if anyone would read it; he just felt like he had to do it to have peace. His first book, *In a Pit with a Lion on a Snowy Day*, was massively successful, as have been all his subsequent books. It is with similar feelings that I am writing this book. I have no idea if anyone will read it, but I feel that I have something to say about this mysterious country that can help people understand it better and appreciate it more. It doesn't really matter to me how successful it is. Like Batterson, I feel compelled to write.

Many people who move to Japan either love it or hate it. My brother, who lived in Tokyo for three years, was one of those who loved it. I remember arguments we used to get into because he would defend everything I thought bizarre or whacked out about Japanese culture. He would say, "Well, it is just the way they do things," or "We don't understand what it is like to be Japanese." I would fire back, "They are some things that are just wrong no matter where you live!" At the other end of the spectrum are foreigners who are unable to adapt to Japan, and as a result, complain all the time. These are foreigners who Cathy Davidson, in her classic book on Japan, *36 Views of Mt. Fuji,* called *gaijin-gaijin* (foreigner-foreigner). These people are constantly comparing Japan to their home countries, and wondering why everything is "wrong". As a teacher of comparative culture, I have learned that in most cases, when talking about cultural differences, it is best and most culturally sensitive to refer to the Japanese way of doing things as "different," not "wrong." I am always correcting my mother for saying, "The Japanese drive on the wrong side of the road."

I have always struggled with trying to discern what differences in the way of doing things are just cultural, and what ways of thinking or behavior are just plain wrong no matter where you live. I have still not answered this question to my satisfaction, but I feel I am getting closer everyday. No doubt my Christian worldview shapes not only who I am but what I believe, so that worldview has influenced what I believe about many of the topics I wrote about in this book.

I have been here for thirteen years and counting. My husband and I have spent all but three of our years together here; my three daughters were born here; my work, church and Japanese family are here. Obviously, I love it here or I would have gone home many years ago like countless *gaijin* before me. Something compels me to stay here. There is something magical about this country that suits me perfectly. I am crazy about it. Yet, there are certain things that drive me crazy. I long to return to family and friends in the U.S., yet when I do, I miss Japan. Every now and then, something will drive me really crazy and I wonder if I even want to stay here. These conflicting feelings motivated me write a book showing what I think is the best and worst of Japan. I have split this book into two sections: in the first section I introduce five things I love about Japan; the second section deals with five things I don't understand. I have not listed them in any particular order of importance--I just wrote as things came to mind and went from there. While I have divided this book into two parts, there is praise, criticism and soul searching in each chapter. This is a complex country, and the issues here are not black and white to me; there is good in the things I don't understand, and there is bad in the things I love. Perhaps many of the topics in this book are familiar to you, but I tried to includes some topics that I have not seen covered very often in other books about Japan.

My desire is everyone reading this book knows that even though I may seem critical at times, I love Japan and the Japanese people with all my heart, and will do so until my dying breath. This country, this culture, and the people who have loved me have captured my heart, and molded me into the person I am today. My hope is that after reading this book, you will have a better understanding of and deeper respect for this mysterious place, and that one day you will visit here and have your life touched by the beautiful Japanese people as I have.

Anne Crescini

Kitakyushu, Japan

December, 2012

Part I:
Five Things I Love

日本の大好きな五つのこと

#1
Onsen and Ofuro

温泉
お風呂

Everybody has seen Hollywood movies where buff jocks are showering with their teammates in the locker room after practice or a big game. Have you ever noticed how you never see girls lathering up in those movies? It is always guys. Girls shower together, too, though. I know, because when I played basketball in college, my teammates always showered together after games. Everyone but me, that is, and a couple of other modest teammates. I am not really sure why even the thought of showering with other girls made me want to break out in hives. Maybe it was due to a poor body image because I was a little overweight. Or maybe it was because we just didn't do that kind of thing in my family. What I do know is that I would have rather stunk to the high heavens than to have had to shower with my teammates. I often wondered if more of my teammates felt the same way, but they just got over it in order to fit in better. I never once took a shower with teammates. After games, I put clean clothes on my sweaty body, and went home and showered in the privacy of my own bathroom. I thought I had escaped the community bathing experience when I put my collegiate sports days behind me. Little did I know that I was destined to spend most of my adult life in the home of naked bathing, the country that has turned bathing into an art, a passion, and a billion-dollar business. At age 23, I was off to Japan, and about to enter the cult of the *onsen*.

The *onsen*, or hot spring, is one of the most popular ways for Japanese people to relax, and an integral part of Japanese culture. They can be found all over Japan, and are probably the number one vacation choice for most Japanese traveling domestically. Certain areas in Japan are particularly famous for their healing waters and delicious foods, and many Japanese will travel hundreds of miles just to enter certain famous *onsens*. They are usually separated into male and female areas, but in some cases you can reserve a private family *onsen*. One thing that makes Japanese hot springs stick out from the hot springs in other countries is that you must bathe naked with strangers, family, and friends (I am not sure which is the worst!) Swimsuits are not allowed. The only covering permitted is a little white towel that many women are delusional enough to think actually covers anything.

I confess that I lived in Japan for three years before I ever went into an *onsen.* If I couldn't even shower with my teammates in the locker room, there was no way I was going to be able to bathe with 90-pound Asian beauties with not even a hint of the saddlebags or cellulite which were so prevalent on my thighs, and on the thighs of every female in my family for ten generations. I did not see any reason to subject myself to that torture, especially since I was heavier at that point than I had been in years. The stress of living in a foreign country, coupled with my hatred of Japanese food was not good for my thighs. I now look at my diet during those days with humor. I never really ate at McDonalds, or consumed a huge quantity of junk food while living in the States, but because it was familiar it became gourmet comfort food once I moved to Japan. That, coupled with the stress of not understanding the language or culture was the perfect recipe for a ten-pound weight gain. Even then, I still only weighed about 147 pounds, a size ten, which is about average in the U.S. But I was fat in Japan, a huge white-skinned American who couldn't even get one leg into the biggest size of Japanese jeans. There was no way I was going to become a naked spectacle at the *onsen.*

Looking back now, I see my fear of *onsens* as three years of wasted opportunity. During that time, I lived twenty minutes from one of the most famous and elegant *onsens* in Japan, Arima Hot Springs in Kobe. There were two things that kept me out of the *onsen* in those days. The first was the overwhelmingly strong conviction that THERE IS NO WAY I AM TAKING A BATH NAKED WITH STRANGERS!!!!! That is putting it lightly. I think most Americans would react the same way I did. While America is an over the top, crazy culture, most people draw a line at taking a bath with strangers. There is a modesty that doesn't really make sense if you think about it within the framework of the rest of the

"Hey, look at me!" attitude that is so prevalent in American culture. I mean, go to any beach and you can look around at all the women wearing virtually nothing. Even on college campuses, there is little modesty when it comes to dress. Many female students, tall or short, overweight or thin, wear Daisy Duke shorts and tank tops to class. But for some reason, being naked in front of those you do not know, and even sometimes, do know, is taboo. I was not any different. I remember the first time I told my mom about a trip to the *onsen*. She promptly called most of my relatives, to inform them of the loopy thing her only daughter had done. You'd have thought I did something wacky like eat raw fish or something...

The second reason is that, at the time, I was just so conscious of sticking out. People were constantly pointing at me and calling me *gaijin* (foreigner). Once a little elementary school boy saw me and ran away screaming, "Foreigner! Foreigner! Ahhhh!!!" I just knew that if I went to an *onsen* while they may not run away screaming, every Japanese in the place would be gawking at the tall, white, chunky foreigner. I know people don't mean to look. They just do. They can't help it. Trust me, because I have been there. Sometimes I find myself looking at other women, comparing my body to theirs, my saddlebags to theirs (I always lose) and I know that I am not the only one who does this. It was hard enough for me to be stared at with clothes on; I just couldn't take being stared at naked. My friends tried to assure me that Japanese people don't pay much attention to others in the *onsen*, that they are shy themselves, but I just couldn't believe it. I found out later that this is actually true; some women are so self-conscious that either they don't go at all, or they go late at night when there is little chance of running into someone they know. For my three years in Kobe, I said a polite "no thank you" and prayed people would stop inviting me.

In 2001, I was living in the U.S. and attending graduate school, and I decided that winter to visit some friends I had met during their semester studying at my university. In the months

17

following the September 11th terror attacks, airfare was dirt-cheap because most people were so scarred by the attacks they were afraid to fly. I managed to find a round-trip ticket from my home in Norfolk, Virginia to Osaka, Japan for $471, which was cheaper than the Gucci bag my friend had just bought in New York. My buddies convinced me to go to Kinosaki Onsen, a famous hot spring in Hyogo Prefecture. Two monumental things happened to me on that trip: I fell in love with *onsens*, and I decided to never have short hair again.

At that time, I was still overweight and terrified of being naked in front of others, but I decided I should at least try it. Although I was overweight, I was a committed Christian who believed it was the inside of a person that really matters, so really, who cares if people look at me? I was comfortable with who I was, and I felt like I should at least try it before I decided I didn't like it. I realized, too, that it is easier being naked with strangers than with friends and family, although I wasn't really looking forward to going with my fashion-model-looking, gorgeous younger friends. I think we think people look at our looks more than we think. Got it? In other words, people are doing their own thing in life. They have better things to do than gawk at each other in the hot spring (although this lady did stare at my youngest Emmy for almost a full minute just the other day. You would have thought she had never seen a white person before!) And if they do gawk at me, who cares? I love me, my family loves me, and God loves me, and I am secure in that.

When I finally took the plunge, I fell in love with it. In the spirit of full disclosure, I must admit that I took off my glasses and I couldn't see a thing. If people were looking at me and my saddlebags, I had no idea. It was maybe one of the first times in my life I was thankful to God and my parents for my dreadful eyesight. I could only see a couple feet (inches?) in front of me, enough to avoid falling and breaking my neck on the wet stones, and I couldn't believe how good the water felt! I remember going back and forth between the scalding hot water and the freezing ice sauna. How had I not done this before? After bathing for an hour or so, we all changed into comfortable *yukata* robes and had a delicious, traditional Japanese meal. Wow. I finally understood what all the fuss was about. It really did feel great to take a bath with strangers!

An onsen in Yufuin, a famous resort in Kyushu.

How long do you think you spend in the shower every morning? I mean, how much time do you really spend washing your body? If most of us are honest, we would probably fess up to a couple of minutes, at most. But let me tell you, Japanese women really know how to clean themselves. I can usually wash my whole body in the time it takes a Japanese woman to wash her left forearm. I am not kidding--they scrub and scrub and scrub. When they are done, they scrub some more. In Japan, you have to thoroughly wash your body and hair before you can enter the *onsen.* You go inside not to get clean, but to relax. It makes sense if you think about it. Why would you want to go into a bath, wash the dirt off, and then soak in dirty, soapy water? It is pretty disgusting if you think about it, and not very relaxing.

The other thing that happened to me during my *onsen* epiphany was that I decided to never have short hair again. Upon arriving at Kinosaki Onsen, I went up to the desk, and the guy there briefly glanced at me and said in Japanese, "Guys to the left." Now, I realize that I had a boyish cut and I am taller and bigger than the average Japanese woman, but I certainly did not look like a man! When I hesitated and he looked at me more closely, he apologized and stuttered all over himself. I got over it, didn't go to the left, but to the right, and started growing my hair out the next day. It has been more than ten years since that first *onsen* trip, but my hair hasn't been cut short since.

It has been a long time since that first trip, and I have a family now. My kids are absolutely crazy about *onsens*. I have three daughters: Mia, who is seven; Abby, who is five; and my baby Emmy, who is three. While they weren't quite so thrilled at the scalding hot water as babies, they love it now. I must admit that I have mixed feelings about the *onsen* at this point in my life. While it still feels heavenly, it is not very relaxing. Up until recently, I couldn't relax or enjoy *onsens* at all due to the fear that my kids would either poop in the water or drown, both of which would have been very bad. Now, I am pretty sure that they will not poop or drown, but I still can't relax because they are so excited they want to move on to a new pool every 38 seconds, and of course I have to follow to make sure they don't poop or drown. Or splash an unsuspecting old lady with water in their excitement. There are rules for *onsen* behavior, and not splashing around like you are in a swimming pool is one of them. At the same time, they are kids, right? *Onsens* are a magical place for kids, and you cannot really expect them to close their eyes and relax, soaking in the magical healing powers for 30 minutes the way that adults would.

Once, my kids were just pouring water from a bucket into the *onsen*, innocently and quietly entertaining themselves, and an *onsen* employee told them to stop playing around. I am very conscious of manners, so if I had thought they were being *meiwaku* (bother or inconvenience) to others, I would have yelled at them myself. Annoyed, I complained at the desk when we were leaving, and was told that sometimes, older guests complain about rowdy kids. Since they are paying money to relax, they don't want to be bothered by kids. I retorted that I was paying, too, and if I had to constantly yell at my kids to stop doing something, I couldn't relax either. So, you can see why *onsens* are not the heavenly bliss they used to be for me. I must admit, though, that I love to see the joy my kids have there. They are so innocent, not at all self-conscious or worried about what others may think of them. Pure. I like that.

About being *meiwaku*, sometimes I think the Japanese spend their entire lives trying to avoid being a bother to others. Because this is such a group-oriented society, all individual actions are expected to be undertaken while considering the impact your actions will have on others. That consideration can be seen in small ways like being quiet on the train and not using your cell phone in public, or in bigger ways like not taking a family vacation because it will inconvenience your co-workers. The concept of *meiwaku* drives personal behavior throughout Japanese culture. Japanese people even have to be considerate when they commit suicide. No kidding. Those who choose to end it all by jumping in front of the train had better think twice, because if they do it this way, their bereaved family may have to pay a fine of thousands of dollars to the train company. Why, you ask? They are being *meiwaku*, of course. Committing suicide by jumping in front of a train causes *meiwaku* to thousands of commuters who will be inconvenienced due to the delay caused by this selfish suicidal act. Of course, with the changing of society and slight shift to individualism in modern Japan, the idea of exactly what constitutes *meiwaku* is changing, but it still dominates the culture. No matter what you do, the number one rule of Japanese culture is this: don't bother or cause trouble to other people. This underlying cultural mantra is why my happy little kids couldn't even play with a bucket in the *onsen*.

One place my kids can have fun without worrying about bothering others is the home version of the *onsen*, the *ofuro*. The closest English translation, I guess would be "bathtub," but oh, no, it is so much more. In recent years, the Japanese, masters of toilet and bathtub technology, have taken the luxury and convenience of the *ofuro* to a whole new level. The single greatest point, one that American makers have yet to duplicate, is the function of keeping the water inside the bath warmed to the same temperature. Have you ever been relaxing in a warm bubble bath only to have the water become cold, forcing you out of the tub shivering? I have. The *ofuro* will maintain the temperature you set it at indefinitely. In fact, some Japanese who really cherish bath time will soak for an hour. Of course, older apartments don't have such modern *ofuros*, but all newer houses and apartments do. I will never forget our first Japanese apartment in Kobe. It only had two small rooms and a kitchen. The bath was old. The kitchen was old. It was such an old apartment that it still had a Japanese-style squatty potty. We had to go to a home center and buy a little plastic toilet adapter to put on top. Voila! A Western toilet! I can make a lot of sacrifices living here, but going without a Western toilet is not one of them. I guess I can't really complain since our rent was only 80 bucks a month.

The *ofuro at* our first place was absolutely the worst. It was a very old-style bath. We first had to fill the tub with cold water. After the tub was full, we had to manually turn a lever to turn on the gas. We could not really control the temperature, so about ten minutes or so after we turned it on, we had to go in and stir the water because the top of the water was hot, but the bottom was still cold. The most frustrating thing was the high level of wrist-flicking skill required to turn it on. There was this little plastic lever that we had to turn halfway, wait for five seconds (not four seconds or six seconds--five), and then with a lightning-quick flick of the wrist turn it back 45 degrees and quickly another 90 degrees in the opposite direction. Confused? We were, too. If the timing at any stage in this process was even a millisecond off, that was too bad for us. It wouldn't turn on. At this point maybe you are saying, "That stinks, but why didn't you just take a shower?" Oh, if it were only that easy. We didn't have a shower. Nope. No shower. We had to use the heated water in the tub and pour it over our heads with a bucket to wash our hair and bodies. So, if we couldn't get the gas to turn on to heat the water, it was either a cold shower (kind of) or no shower. I can't count how many times I chose the latter. I gave up, and went into the kitchen to at least wash my hair in the kitchen sink. The gas there was easy to turn on, and did not carry the risk of a wrist injury.

Our ofuro: Respite from the cold.

In our new place in Kitakyushu, however, we realized we had come a long way when we saw how cool and easy to operate our *ofuro* was. This is what gave me the most joy when I looked at our place for the first time. I didn't care so much that it was small and old. It had a modern *ofuro* and Western toilet, so I was all set. My kids love hanging out in the *ofuro* like they do the *onsen*, and they have been spoiled by it. I remember a couple years ago, we visited the U.S. for Christmas for the first time in seven years. Up until that point, we had always traveled home during the summer. While we had a blast seeing family and friends, one of the hardest things for us in the U.S. was bath time. The kids were not old enough yet for showers, and were still scared of getting water on their faces. But it seemed that many of the places we stayed had a limited supply of hot water for baths. I remember panicking, feeling like my kids were on an assembly line trying to get them in and out before the water got too cold. They were miserable, and I was stressed out. Everybody hated bath time. Of course, American kids don't know any better because that's all they have ever known. But my kids, who were spoiled by the Japanese *ofuro,* were traumatized.

My personal favorite *ofuro* function is the tub announcing to me, "Your bath is now ready" ten minutes after pushing only one button and leaving it to prepare itself for me.   This is after two minutes earlier telling me that my bath water is almost ready. Because Japanese houses are so cold (I will get to that later), the *ofuro* is one place to go to escape the frigid temperatures and relax after a long day at work. Most Japanese bathe at night, not in the mornings, like Americans. It is not for them solely a way to clean the body, but to refresh the soul. It is a relaxing end to a busy, stressful day. While many Americans feel cruddy waking up and going out without showering, most Japanese think it is disgusting to go to bed dirty. Going to bed dirty is no problem for me; if I took at bath at night, my hair would be quite a sight to behold the following morning. I finally figured out after years in Japan that Japanese bathing habits are the main reason that gyms don't open before ten a.m. People don't work out in the morning because they bathe at night. Who wants to get sweaty and have to take a shower before work after getting so clean the night before? Not most Japanese.

Bathing in Japan is a national obsession. It begins shortly after birth, with the newborn baby scrubbed clean of the afterbirth just hours after arriving, continuing with a daily scouring until mother and child are discharged. I remember watching the midwives give a bath to one of my daughters a couple of days after birth. I thought they were going to scrub her skin raw. I mean, how dirty can a newborn get during the course of the day? In fact, Americans don't even give babies a real bath until after the umbilical cord stump falls off, usually a couple weeks after birth.

Not the Japanese. I am 99.9% sure that not a day goes by from birth to college that the average Japanese kid doesn't take a bath. Of course, busy college students and singles with small apartments often forgo the *ofuro* for the Western shower, but the majority of Japanese still take an *ofuro* every night. I am amazed how my mommy friends whose husbands work late give their kids a bath every night, without fail: summer, winter, sickness, health. No matter what. Only for certain illnesses is the nightly *ofuro* skipped. We usually give our kids a bath every day during summer, but as sloppy Americans, during winter it is usually reduced to every three days, or when there is so much food in their hair that I cannot comb it, whichever comes first.

The kids love the *ofuro*, but honestly, it can be a hassle. Whereas in the U.S. most parents hang out beside the tub and wash their kids, in Japan, parents get in the tub and bathe with their kids. Just like in the *onsen*, everyone must wash off with soap and water, as well as shampoo their hair before entering the *ofuro*. Many Japanese tubs are square-shaped and deep, so it is difficult for parents to bathe young children without getting in with them. The shower head is outside the tub in the same room, so everyone showers, and then hops in the tub. The fact that we as parents have to get in with our kids is sometimes both stressful and time-consuming. I am a morning person, waking up at 4 am, so by the time bath time rolls around I am tired and already in my pajamas. I don't feel like undressing, showering and getting in the tub. Unlike most people here, I like to exercise in the mornings, so I shower in the mornings. Usually, my husband will do bath time, like most Japanese daddies (This is considered one of the major child raising responsibilities of Japanese fathers. My husband, of course, contributes much more than this!) I used to dry the kids off and dress them, but they can do that by themselves now. My oldest daughter is now able to take a shower by herself, although she still prefers we get in tub with her. However, we are starting to think about how much longer my girls and husband should see each other naked; many Japanese girls will take baths with their fathers until the end of elementary school.

As much as the *ofuro* can be annoying sometimes with its time-consuming nature, it is truly heaven and one of the greatest inventions the Japanese have given the world. There is nothing like soaking in a toasty bath on a freezing winter day, and playing with kids in the tub on the weekends when things are not quite so hectic. I think if my family ever moves back to the U.S., we will seriously consider paying out the nose to import and install a Japanese-style tub, unless of course, the U.S. catches on by then. I doubt it, because bathing is just not the cultural obsession that it is here. I am not sure if it is because of or in spite of the busyness of this culture that bath time is so sacred. Maybe a little of both. All I know, is that this is one part of the culture that my family has embraced, and is absolutely crazy about.

#2
The Health Care System

医療制度

My second daughter, Abby, has always been so unique. She is sensitive, cries at the drop of a hat, and is incredibly goofy, much like me actually. Developmentally, she has been stuttering in both languages since the age of three, and she seems a little behind other kids her age. At this point, we are not worried about her; in fact, her stutter seems to be getting better lately. She loves to learn new things, so we think with a little extra effort on our part, she will catch up with other kids her age in no time. One thing that especially sets her apart from her sisters is her sensitivity to touch and smell. She is always holding and collecting things (she is a future star of the reality show *Hoarders*). She comforted herself when she was little by holding a towel up to her nose and smelling it. Recently, she has exchanged the towel for her 12-member finger puppet family, which she carries everywhere with her. They are all amusingly enough named "Mr. Mouse," even though not one of them is an actual mouse. There are pigs, cows, rabbits, snakes, horses, dogs, and cats. But no mice.

The thing that I love the most is how she loves my hair. For the past two or three years, whenever Abby has been tired or scared or upset, she has crawled up into my lap and grabbed my hair (which is getting more forceful and painful as she gets older) and started sniffing. She takes it and smells it, touching it to her nose. No matter how upset she is or how much serious crying has been going on, this will always calm her down immediately. She loves my hair so much that I have purposely not cut it too short so she always has long enough hair to grab and smell. Sometimes she will come to me for a pit stop while playing, take a whiff, and be on her way. Recently, she has even started saying goodbye to my hair in the mornings before we drop her off at preschool. While my hair is her favorite, she has also been known to follow little sister Emmy around smelling her hair, too, as she walks. It's a quite a sight, but Emmy doesn't seem to appreciate it like I do. I must admit that I love that Abby loves my hair and finds such comfort in it, and I am not looking forward to the day when she doesn't need it anymore. My husband, Riz, and I often wonder if all these little things that make Abby so unique might be attributed to a big health scare she had as a baby.

When Abby was eight months old, she suffered a febrile seizure. For those unfamiliar with this, it is a fever-induced seizure relatively common in young children. Up to 10% of children suffer a febrile seizure early in life, most commonly before the age of three. While they are extremely scary to watch, most of these seizures are harmless and have no lasting effects on the child. However, in Abby's case, things were a little different.

One Friday morning in May, Abby woke up acting like her usual cheerful self. From birth, she had been an incredibly easy and happy baby, pretty much doing nothing but sleeping, eating, and laughing all day long. We took her to preschool as usual, but after lunch we got a call that she was running a fever, and that we should come and get her. We had gotten calls like this all the time about our older daughter Mia, and she always seemed to be fine when we got there. We picked Abby up and she was a little warm, but other than that, seemed fine. We took her to our weekly church café, and put her down for a nap in the kids' room. When she woke up in the early evening, she was burning up and listless. This was her first fever, but we were not that worried. I mean, kids get fevers all the time, right? However, since her fever was 39.7 C (103.5 F) and it was Friday night, we decided we should take her to the emergency room just to be on the safe side.

We got there and the doctor saw her within an hour. He examined her, said it was some kind of virus but hard to tell what, and said he would prescribe some antibiotics. While we were waiting in the waiting room, Abby started shaking in my arms. I had never seen a seizure before, but had heard of febrile seizures from one of the many baby books I had read to prepare for parenthood. So, I went and got a nurse immediately all the while trying to stay calm. They took her into the examination room and asked us to wait outside. It was the longest 30 minutes of my life. I had no idea what was going on, no idea if she was going to be okay, and no one would tell us anything. People were running in and out of the room, monitors were beeping. I was absolutely terrified. How could my smiling, happy baby who was fine this morning go south so fast? I felt powerless, helpless and afraid. Riz and I just prayed. We prayed, and we called friends and family and asked them to pray, too.

A half an hour later, Abby was wheeled out on a stretcher, with tubes and monitors connected everywhere. I'll never forget the sight of her tiny hand flailing in the air and still twitching, even though she was unconscious. I asked the nurses what was going on, if Abby was going to be okay, and they kept saying, "We cannot say anything at this point. The doctor will talk to you soon." That made me even more terrified. The Japanese have perfected the art of the poker face. I couldn't tell anything from her reaction, but the fact that the nurses wouldn't even say that she was okay for now freaked me out. They told me that they were taking her for a CT scan, and that we should come along. We waited for the scan to be finished and waited to talk to the doctor. Waiting, waiting, waiting. There is nothing worse than waiting, especially when it is waiting for news of your child and knowing there is nothing you can do as a parent to help.

When the doctor finally talked to us, he informed us that Abby had had a complex febrile seizure. Seizures in young children usually last less than five minutes, but in Abby's case, had lasted 30 minutes. This is highly unusual, so they wanted to hospitalize Abby to run tests and monitor her to make sure that she had no more seizures. While we were relieved that she was out of immediate danger, there were still so many unknowns. Would she have another seizure? Would she have any adverse effects of the seizure? When would she wake up? She was still sedated and sleeping when she finished her CT scan, with just an occasional jerk or twitch, signs that it was a pretty serious seizure. I settled in to her private room, which is unusual in Japan due the nature of the national health care system; most people stay in rooms with at least three other people. I still am not sure why they gave us a private room, but am grateful for it.   I prepared myself for an unexpected, indefinite hospital stay.

Japanese moms almost always stay with their hospitalized kids 24 hours a day, with the exception of getting some needed breaks from family members and friends. The cool thing is, there is this giant crib where mother and child sleep together. It looks like something out of a fairy tale, a crib for giants or something. This is a much better setup than in most U.S. hospitals where, many times family members must sleep in chairs or on the sofa. Abby didn't sleep very well those first few nights; she finally woke up and seemed okay, but there was this hollow, glassy look in her eyes. The doctors told me that this was the result of the seizure and medication that they were giving her, but I wanted to cry every time I looked at her. In fact, one of my friends burst into tears when she saw Abby for the first time after her seizure. She looked so much unlike the happy, energetic baby I had seen just a few days before. She had monitors, IVs and tubes hooked up to check for a possible second seizure, so the monitor was constantly beeping and waking her up. Although she had a big appetite and ate and nursed well, her fever would spike everyday in the evening. This went on for three days, and we still had no idea what had caused the seizure or the fever.

Finally, on day three, she developed a rash on her body, and doctors diagnosed *roseola* virus. She started to feel better from that point and gradually started acting like her old self. At the end of day three, her fever finally broke. We stayed a few more days for observation, and she was released a week after being hospitalized. We were told to come back in a couple weeks for a follow up EEG to make sure that she did not have epilepsy. In addition, she had to take anti-seizure meds every time her fever spiked above 37.5 C (99.5 F) until she was three years old. We learned that with complex febrile seizures, there is a 50% chance of reoccurrence, so parents must be vigilant with all fevers, no matter how slight.

Imagine my shock when we checked out and had to pay a grand total of $39. Are you kidding me? One week in the hospital in a private room, a battery of tests, monitors, and medication and we only had to pay $39?? What a country! I found out later that this $39 was to pay for her meals, the only thing that national health care doesn't pay for in Kitakyushu city for preschool age kids. Each city in Japan has a different standard for covering health care costs for children, but in Kitakyushu, all medical care for kids is free until they enter elementary school, at which time parents have to pay the same costs they pay for themselves under the national health care system.

Mommy with Abby in her giant hospital bed after her seizure.

This level of health care at such a cost is unheard of in the U.S., where there are many uninsured kids, and parents struggle to give them adequate medical care. All immunizations are covered as well, with the exception of mumps, flu, and chicken pox. In fact, many Japanese parents do not immunize their kids against these sicknesses, partly because they don't want to pay almost $100 for one shot, and partly because they think it is normal for their kids to get these diseases during childhood. I personally think that because Japanese parents don't know any other system, they don't have anything to compare it to. They don't realize how wonderful the Japanese health care system is, especially regarding the treatment of children. I used to not even take my wallet to the doctor's office, but unfortunately, I had to start paying for the oldest on April 1, 2012, the date she entered elementary school. The first time I took her to the doctor after that, I had to pay about nine bucks, which in my new altered reality here in Japan seemed like a small fortune.

Of course, anything that is free has the potential for abuse. Japanese parents take their kids to the doctor way sooner than American parents would, and for much less serious illnesses. Granted, there are very few over-the-counter medications for children sold in Japanese pharmacies, so parents rarely make decisions about how to medicate their children. My sister-in-law in the States tells me she gives her kids a fever reducer and keeps an eye on them for three days before calling the doctor. In the U.S. not only is the pediatrician expensive, appointments are hard to come by, and the waiting time is long and often unpredictable. Here, my kids can be in and out of the doctor in ten minutes with no appointment.

After Mia was born, since I was both new to parenting and to taking care of sick kids, I would rush her to the doctor at the slightest sign of illness, including cough and runny nose. Many parents do the same here, although I am sure that parents wouldn't do this quite so often if they had to pay. Now, two kids later, I am a little wiser and less prone to panicking, so I usually don't take my kids to the doctor unless they have high fevers or persistent coughs. There is no need for them to take unnecessary medication or risk catching any one of the other myriad of germs sure to be floating around the pediatrician's office. Most of the times they have fevers, they are better the next day with no treatment anyway. In fact, I cannot think of one time my kids have gone to bed with a fever and still had it the next morning. So, even though free medical care for my kids is a huge comfort, I still don't want them taking medicine they don't really need or unnecessarily exposing them to germs. Germs are a funny thing. When the swine flu was going around, I was a crazy militant "Don't you dare eat that without washing your hands!" kind of mommy; I never left the house with out my mini hand sanitizer. They all caught the swine flu anyway (although Mia was running around the house singing Jingle Bells after only one dose of Tamiflu!) The next year, they never washed their hands and didn't get sick at all. Go figure. I still have to believe that washing your hands has to be a better bet than not washing them, though.

Medical care for adults in Japan is more expensive but still incredibly reasonable. The cheap fees and aging population have led the system into the red, so the Japanese government has raised the out-of-pocket expenses from ten percent to thirty percent in recent years. This is on top of a monthly premium paid, so the Japanese system is not pure socialism like can be found in many European countries. I don't think most U.S. citizens would be opposed to a Japanese-style health insurance system. However, the reasonable cost does cause some problems. The elderly in Japan (everybody knows the Japanese live forever!) use health insurance more than any other group, and they pay the least, so this is putting a significant strain on the system. My friends tell me that the elderly love going to the hospital to hang out with their friends, and that some like to go socialize everyday. With Japan's population expected to drop 30% in the next 40 years due to the aging population and declining birthrate, further changes in the existing system are bound to be necessary at some point.

But for now, I only pay about $150 a month for medical care for my entire family. There are two types of national health insurance; social insurance (*shakai hoken*), for which half of the fee is subsidized by the employer; and citizen's insurance (*kokumin hoken*), which is paid for entirely by the individual. The monthly premium for citizen's insurance is based on income from the previous year. Regardless of which of the two systems one is enrolled in, the benefits, out-of-pocket expenses, and accessibility are the same. My monthly social insurance premium of $110 plus thirty percent out-of-pocket may sound like a lot, but the cost of everything, including office visits, tests and medication, is cheaper here. Consider this example: My husband had a colonoscopy recently, and his out-of-pocket expenses were only $100. Now, I have about a third-grade math level, maybe worse, but I am still pretty sure that this means that with no insurance, the cost would be a little over $300. This test would easily cost over $1000 in the U.S. A simple office visit usually costs between $2 and $10 with insurance in Japan.

Not only is health care cheap, it is highly accessible to all. There are no primary care physicians, or referrals like in the U.S. If you are enrolled in the national health plan, you can go directly to any doctor or dentist. Some big university hospitals will charge you more with no referral, but you can still see a doctor there. The best part is that not only big hospitals, but also many small clinics will have expensive testing equipment so you can have a test done on the same day as your office visit with no wait.

When my oldest daughter was a baby, I threw out my back doing something very strenuous--reaching for my computer. Just kidding. Not about reaching for the computer, but about it being strenuous. It was a pretty embarrassing way to throw out my back, but the sad reality is that I am no spring chicken anymore. Anyway, I was in incredible pain and could not nurse my daughter without lying down. I could not even get out of bed by myself. We slept on a futon on the floor, so it was even harder to get up than if I had been in a bed. That night, in the middle of the night, I had to go to the bathroom, so I woke my husband up and asked him to help me get there. My last memory is of feeling dizzy. I woke up about a minute later, having passed out from the pain in the bathroom. My husband said I was groaning and mumbling, my eyes were glassed over, and he was about to call the ambulance when I finally came to. It was a scary experience, but not a new one. I passed out a lot as a kid. Once I passed out at church when I was an acolyte and hit my head on the communion rail.

That was almost as dramatic as the time I passed out at a baseball game standing in line for concessions. Luckily, I fell on top of two little kids and they broke my fall. My wooziness certainly makes for good stories at least. My favorite fainting spell happened right after I came to Japan. I passed out on the train on the way home from work, my last thought being how awful the cheese bread I was eating tasted. I woke up on the floor of a crowded Japanese train during rush hour, with 20 pairs of eyes on me, and the mouths connected to them all asking me if I was *daijoubu?* (OK?) Well, I guess that is one unconventional way to get a seat on a crowded rush hour train.

This time was a little different, though. I was unconscious for a while, and groaning, so I thought I should go to see a neurosurgeon and get an MRI just to be safe. Of course, in the U.S., I would first have to go see my primary care doctor, and he would refer me to the neurosurgeon if he thought it was necessary. Then I would have to wait weeks, maybe months to get an appointment.

But in Japan, I just thought, "Gee, I should visit a neurosurgeon" and off I went. Even though I didn't have an appointment, I waited only a half an hour or so to see the doctor, and then explained to him what had happened. He said, "Let's do an MRI." I said, "Now?" He replied, "Sure. I have a machine here." In the U.S. no private doctor would have an MRI machine in his office, since it costs more than a million dollars. When I told my family doctor in the U.S this story he couldn't believe it. I had the MRI, got the results (I was fine) and was out in an hour, paying my share of 30%, which was about $50.00 Being a compulsive worrier, I love that fact that here I can get a test done pretty quickly, not having to wait for the test and wait some more for the results. Once I even had a colonoscopy performed same day, with no appointment. (I wasn't planning on that one!). Of course, if you go to a big university hospital, you may have to wait, but there are usually small clinics everywhere that can do the same kinds of tests.

Another thing I love is the Special Chronic Disease Program (*tokutei shikkan*) that I am enrolled in. I have had ulcerative colitis since I was in college, and because of this program, all of my medication is free. This helps a lot, since it would cost at least $50 a month out-of-pocket for my regular medication, and more for the steroids I need for occasional flare-ups. I don't have to pay more than $50 a month for outpatient treatment, or $100 a month for hospitalization related to my disease. I wish I had known about this program during the three years I lived in Kobe, but nobody ever told me about it. There are so many benefits like this program available in Japan if you just know about them. There are 56 chronic diseases on this list, and most people with these conditions are approved if their doctor certifies their illness. The paperwork is a yearly pain in the neck, but it is more than worth it.

There are a lot of humorous things about the health care system, too. There is a lottery every year for free health check-ups at work. The Japanese love lotteries. My brother recently won a lottery to run in the Tokyo Marathon. I remember thinking after winning a lottery for an extensive health check how maybe someone who doesn't win the health check-up lottery may die of an undiscovered disease. It's humorous if you think about the logic. I have won three health check-ups so far (what luck!): one extensive check, one for female cancers, and one for my husband as my dependent. Those who don't win the lottery or choose not to enter are required by their workplace to undergo a basic health check-up every year, paid for by their employer. It covers things like blood and urine tests, EKG, chest x-ray, vision and hearing tests, and weight check. But if you want more extensive tests like abdominal ultrasound, echocardiogram, or mammography, you have to win the lottery.

I think I have had almost every test known to man done at Japanese hospitals. I have had a spinal tap, CT scan, MRI, chest x-ray, EKG, 24-hour EKG, echocardiogram, abdominal ultrasound, lymph node ultrasound, and mammogram. I joke with my husband that my medical Japanese is better than most Japanese people. I am only partly joking; I think I really do believe it. In fact, I remember talking to one of my students once in Japanese and telling her I had meningitis, and she was like, "What's that?" I am more knowledgeable about the Japanese medical system than I am about perhaps any other aspect of Japanese life. I know how to save money on hospitalization. I know where all the good doctors are with the shortest waits and best machines. Of course, being sickly is annoying and discouraging at times, but it has given me the knowledge to help other people, and I am thankful for that.

I don't think the Japanese medical system is perfect. It has flaws. Until recently, children could not be organ donors, and as a result, organ recipients. This led desperate parents overseas, incurring not only huge financial debt, but also the wrath of local parents whose children got pushed lower down on the waiting list by the Japanese children. Organ transplants are still not really understood, so this system, even for adults lags greatly behind other countries. I am not an expert, but I hear that cancer treatment is also not very aggressive. It is kind of a "Let's wait and see if that tumor gets any bigger" kind approach. OF COURSE IT WILL GET BIGGER!! GET IT OUT OF ME!! So, as long as I do not need an organ transplant or get stricken with cancer, Japan is the place for me.

Another small annoyance is that, in order for doctors to milk the government out of as much money as they can, the number of visits required for the treatment of an illness is unbelievable. It takes nine visits and more than two months to have a root canal. I know, because my kids and I have combined for at least ten of them (I blame the lack of fluoride in the tap water, but it is more likely the cotton candy and cookies). It takes two visits for a dental cleaning; and if you have some kind of ENT-related issue like a sinus infection, hay fever or allergies, you will probably go several times a week for eternity. Maybe that is a slight exaggeration, but not much of one. The Japanese have this term, "*byoin ni kayou*," which means, "to commute to the hospital." They ain't kidding.

When I was pregnant, I got several sinus infections. Most people know that sinus infections require antibiotics to clear up, but Japanese doctors are terrified to give medication to pregnant women. They won't do it, partly because of not wanting to take responsibility, partly because of a stubborn misconception here that all medication is dangerous in pregnancy. Of course, my OB had no trouble doling out the drugs. I felt like they gave it out like candy—antibiotics, laxatives, cold medicine, headache medication, fever reducers. My doctor told me most medications are safe during pregnancy-- even anti-anxiety drugs are okay outside the first trimester. But since specialists won't give you medicine, and the OB doesn't know what is wrong with you, you must first go to the specialist, get him to confirm what you probably already know is wrong with you, and then go back to the OB and tell him what the specialist said. The OB will then proceed to give you the necessary medication for your condition. So, when I had my sinus infection, the ENT wouldn't give me medication, he just wanted me to wash my nose. So I had do get antibiotics at the OB.

Huh? Wait a minute. Did I just say wash my nose? That's right. Nose washing is one of the weirdest, but strangely most refreshing medical treatments in Japan. This treatment is common for a variety of ENT ailments, from sinus infections to colds, to allergies. The nurse squirts water up one nostril while holding the other one shut, and you snort it out like blowing your nose into this metal pan that she holds for you. At first, it feels pretty gross and uncomfortable, kind of like getting water up your nose when swimming. But after you are finished, it feels great! There is nothing like the feeling immediately after nose washing. No matter how stuffed up you might have been, your nasal passages are clear and stinging like you just squirted a whole bottle of nose spray up there. It feels so great that it is addicting. Most doctors want patients to commute and wash their noses a few days a week for a few weeks, until their symptoms get better. Many times they will do this instead of, or along with, medication. They think this is the best path for pregnant women because it helps avoid medication. I guess it does work eventually, but it is so much slower than drugs.

My first ENT in Japan was like a medieval torture chamber. The machines looked so old and archaic. One of my most painful experiences was some kind of sinus infection treatment where the doctor put this long device up my nose, supposedly to clear the passage between my nasal cavity and ear canal. It felt like that needle was snaking its way all the way to my ear. After the procedure was finished, I listened shell-shocked as he explained that intense pain was probably due to my high Western nose. Sure, doc, blame my nose and not your way outdated torture techniques. Unlike nose washing, that one didn't even help all that much. Japanese people are obsessed with the so-called Western high nose. People always remark how my kids have a high nose even though they don't; they have my husband's Southeast Asian pug nose. I guess they just assume because they have white skin, they must have a high nose. There are a few comments that we have heard a couple hundred times since my kids were born. I will give them to you here in order of frequency:

#1 "Oh my goodness ! How cute!"

#2 "Oh, she looks like a doll!"

#3 "What long eyelashes!"

#4 "Look at that high nose!"

Anyway, I never had to have the high nose-induced torture again, but I did have to commute often for nose washing. I often wondered how the Japanese, some of the busiest people in the world, had the time to commute to the hospital. One way is their ingenious strategy to reduce waiting time. Most clinics in Japan don't take appointments, so it is a first come, first served system. Without a strategy, you could end up waiting for hours.

The first time I visited the most popular ENT in town, I was pleasantly surprised that there was only a handful of people in the waiting room. This shouldn't take long, I thought. Ha! Two hours later, I was still waiting. Name after name was called, but not mine. Where are all these phantom patients coming from anyway, I thought? I finally figured it out. People had come in earlier and written their names. They estimated about when they would be called and came back. I thought this was a pretty sneaky thing to do, but then I realized it is sanctioned by the hospital. In fact, most hospitals open early just for people to sign in. Of course, it is a little risky. If your name is called and you are not there, you get skipped and have to start all over again. One time, I went to this same hospital early Saturday morning to get my name on that list. The office opened at 9 am, and I was there at 8:15, thinking I was pretty smart to get there that early. Imagine my shock when I saw 57 people had already written their names. Are you kidding me? What time did this list get placed out here anyway? I wrote my name, thinking it would be at least an hour and a half before they got to me. I asked the receptionist what time I should come back, and she said 9:30. I laughed at the ridiculousness that the doctor could see 57 people in 30 minutes, but I didn't want to miss my turn and have to be behind 200 people, so I came back just a little later, around 9:45. They were already to number 50. Unbelievable. I had barely made it back in time. There was something a little disturbing about a doctor who could see 50 people in 45 minutes. Later, I found out some patients probably just needed medicine or nose washing, so they didn't need to actually see the doctor. I was a little jealous of those lucky ones getting to wash their noses...

Financially, you will never go broke in Japan due to illness, an occurrence that is unfortunately very common in the U.S. But a person without a lot of knowledge of the system will pay more than necessary. In Japan, those enrolled in the National Healthcare System will never be required to pay more than 80,100 yen a month (800 dollars) out-of-pocket for health-related expenses. This system, (called *kogaku iryou* in Japanese), includes hospitalization, surgery or any testing. You can even claim this on your taxes and get some of it back later. Most people add hospitalization riders to their life insurance policies as well, meaning that they will get 5000-10,000 yen ($50-$100) a day per hospitalization. This is their way to ensure that not only will they not go broke, but they will not lose any money at all. In fact, in some cases, people will actually make a profit on illness or surgery.

This is a great system, but one that I wish someone had told me more about it when I first arrived in Japan. The one-month period is a calendar month, which means, for example, I will not have to pay more than 80,100 yen in May. Of course, if one has an emergency illness or is involved in an accident, the dates and times of the hospitalization cannot be controlled. However, if it is an elective surgery, a person would be wise to schedule it so that hospitalization falls entirely within one calendar month to save money. It is possible to pay twice as much for a one-week hospital stay than a 30-day stay if you are not careful.

Riz tore his ACL and needed surgery to repair it. While in the U.S. this requires only a day or two stay in the hospital, in Japan patients must stay 2-4 weeks, depending on the hospital and the doctor. The thinking in the U.S. is if there is no chance you will die, you need to be discharged, most of the time because insurance companies don't want to pay any more than they have to. After all, rehab can easily be done on an outpatient basis. In Japan, however, the overriding idea is that patients not be discharged until they are totally healed and ready to take care of themselves. For orthopedic surgeries, many doctors want patients to do the majority of their rehab in the hospital before discharge. Of course, this is due to the massive difference between private and government-sponsored health care.

We were unaware of the system to cap payment at 80,100 yen a month, so we scheduled his surgery for the end of February and beginning of March. He was in the hospital only two weeks, but we had to pay 80,100 yen for February, and 80,100 yen for March. If I had realized scheduling the surgery in one calendar month would have saved us $800, of course that is what I would have done. These are the kinds of things that you never see written about in books about Japan, and hospitals will never tell you; you only learn about them through experience. Of course, again, you do not have this luxury when unexpected illness strikes. When my oldest Mia was a baby, I contracted meningitis and was hospitalized for only a week, but unfortunately, it was at the end of July and early August. So, even though I was only in the hospital a week, I ended up paying 160,200 yen. The *kogaku iryou* system guards against individual bankruptcy, and is a great help and comfort, especially if one knows how to use it to one's advantage, but it does seem a little unfair at times.

One aspect of the medical system I am absolutely not crazy about is emergency care. When Emmy was almost two, the girls and I were all taking a bath one night, just relaxing and having fun playing together. It was the middle of May, and the weather was getting warmer. The bath was really hot, so I turned on the cold water to cool off the water a bit. Emmy, at that time, loved to drink the water, so she kept trying to lap up the water like a dog on a hot summer day. Before I realized it, when I looked at her, she had the faucet in her mouth drinking the water. I started to panic thinking that she might drown herself, so I tried to take the faucet out of her mouth. I am a little fuzzy about what happened next, but I think that she bit down on it, making it even more difficult to remove. Looking back, all I had to do was turn off the water.

Unfortunately, parents do not have the luxury of calm thinking and hindsight when they are panicking about their child's safety.

Anyway, I was really freaking out at this point. I couldn't take the faucet out of her mouth, so I yanked hard to get it out. This finally got the faucet out of her mouth, along with some other stuff that wasn't supposed to come out. There was blood everywhere, her back molar was hanging by a thread, and everyone was screaming and crying; Emmy, because she was in pain; Mommy because I was freaked out and panicking; and Mia and Abby because they were terrified by all the blood. I screamed for Riz and he came and tried to stop the bleeding. We didn't know what to do because we did not know how bad the injury was. Mouth wounds bleed like crazy, so there was a lot of blood. We decided to call an ambulance, but we looked around frantically (I was still naked) for our cell phones but couldn't find them anywhere, causing us to panic even more. Finally, we found my phone, called the ambulance, and waited. I put on some clothes while Riz held Emmy, who was whimpering by now but calmed down. We still did not know where exactly all the blood was coming from. Mia and Abby were still crying hysterically. I remember Mia going to get an iPhone. She opened up the photo folder and kept crying, "I love Emmy! I don't want her to die."

Emmy's right molar: out eight years too early.

44

Well, up to this point, it was a traumatic experience emotionally to say the least, but nothing to really complain about yet as far as the medical system goes. The ambulance arrived quickly and I explained what had happened. Emmy and I got into the ambulance, and Riz and the other girls stayed behind. The paramedic asked me, "Which hospital do you want to go to?" Huh, I thought? You are the paramedic. You should know where is the best and fastest place to go. You don't ask a panicking mommy to make such a calm, rational decision. But I answered with the name of the only hospital we had ever been to for pediatric emergency because I did not know anywhere else. It seemed to take forever, but in reality we arrived in ten or fifteen minutes. The whole time the paramedic is telling me to be careful that Emmy not swallow her tooth, since it is still hanging by a thread. Apparently, there is the possibility that the tooth may enter the lung and cause major problems if swallowed.

We arrived at the hospital, were ushered into the examination room, and the paramedic took her leave after explaining the facts to the doctor. The doctor then proceeded to tell us that yes, Emmy's back molar was hanging by a thread, and no, there seem to be no further injuries. This was a relief, but I was shocked at what she said next: "Unfortunately, we do not have emergency dentistry at this hospital, so you have to go somewhere else." WHAT?? We came all the way here, and there is no doctor that can help Emmy? Why did the paramedic in the ambulance not know that there is no dentistry at this hospital? Isn't that her job? Why did she not tell me? Why did they take me somewhere they knew couldn't help? Are the Japanese so obedient that they do what the customer (patient) says, even if they know better? There were so many outrageous thoughts going through my head. Meanwhile, Emmy's tooth is still hanging by a thread, and I am still try to make sure that she didn't swallow it. I have no way to get to another hospital because I had, duh, come by ambulance. So, I am holding a heavy baby with a potentially life-threatening dangling tooth in a way so she wouldn't swallow it while trying to call another hospital to see if they would see Emmy. The first hospital wouldn't even call for us; they just gave us a number. In addition, I had no way to get there, so I had to call someone to come pick us up. We finally found a hospital that would see us, and our close friend, Mrs. Ito, came to get us. Unfortunately, by the time we saw the emergency dentist, two hours had passed. The doctor tried to put the tooth back, but in the two hours we were trying to find a hospital, the blood started clotting, so it was impossible. He ended up pulling the tooth, so Emmy will be minus a chomper until she is about ten. The dentist said he thinks he could have saved the tooth had we gotten there sooner.

I am so thankful that Emmy was not hurt more seriously. In fact, by the time we were in the car headed to the second hospital, she was fine, cheerfully bouncing all around the car. This was tough for me, as I was happy she was feeling better, but still trying to keep that life-threatening missile out of her lungs! She only cried when the doctor was yanking on her tooth. I am thankful, but I am also flabbergasted at the emergency response. I just can't believe that the ambulance took me to a hospital that couldn't help me, and then stranded me there without any way to get to a place that could. I had often heard negative stories on the news about emergency care, but had never really had a negative experience myself. Often, pregnant women who have complications are driven around in an ambulance for hours because they are turned down by emergency room after emergency room. Apparently, a hospital will not see a pregnant woman in an emergency situation if she has not yet had her first pregnancy checkup there. You can see the problems this would cause if a woman has complications before she knows she is pregnant or before she has been to the obstetrician. She is in no-man's land. I think ultimately the problem lies in a lack of doctors in emergency care, and a shortage of beds if that person needs to be admitted. But what about the paramedics? What's the deal with them?

The day after the accident, a nurse that goes to my church told me that the hospital five minutes from my house has emergency dentistry. I couldn't help but laugh at the irony, and wonder why the paramedic didn't recommend that hospital to me. I also learned that Japanese paramedics do not have near the training that paramedics have in the States. More than anything, they are transporters of sick people. The lack of knowledge and confidence was more than a little disturbing, and I have seen the lack of decision-making many times in Japanese medical professionals. When Abby was hospitalized with her seizure, her doctor just seemed to keep saying, "I wonder if she will be okay." Or "I think this will work." Or "Yeah, maybe I will try this." Or "I wonder why this is happening." I don't want my doctor to wonder; I want him to know. Or at least to act like he knows. There is nothing worse than talking to a doctor with no confidence in what he is doing or no advice about how to make things better.

I have had 13 or so (who's counting?) colonoscopies in my life, at least half of them in Japan. While in the U.S., I did all the test preparation at home the day before, in Japan most people arrive early in the morning at the hospital, start drinking two liters of the super strength laxative, and make small talk with the other patients about their bowel movements. People in this country love talking about bowel movements; maybe because it is a sign of good health or something, and those waiting around to have a colonoscopy are even more prone to share too much information. In order to do the test, you have to get the all clear from the nurse, who checks your poop usually a couple hours after the drinking commences. Patients willingly share their success or failure with each other like, "Well, I'm almost there. Still a little too muddy, I think," or "Maybe one more time will do it for me!" or "Yeah! I passed!" Bowel movements tend to be a more of a private matter in the U.S., but they seem to be eagerly discussed here, and nowhere more than in that little room full of mostly older people getting ready for a colonoscopy.

For some reason, the bowel cleansing, foul-tasting concoction they use here seems to work on everyone but me. Nobody seems to know why, including my doctor. I think I am a legend at the hospital. They probably say, "Here comes the foreigner with the laxative-resistant bowels!" For the most recent colonoscopy last year, I drank two liters the night before, and an additional two liters the morning of the test. I mean, that stuff is foul. Just thinking about it as I write makes me want to hurl. But alas, not even four liters did the trick. I wistfully watched the little room empty as person after person got the thumbs up from the nurses and headed off for the test. I never did get the all clear, but since the hospital was about to shut down for the day, the doctor had to do the test anyway, almost twenty hours after the test prep marathon had started. I was hungry, nauseous, and had a splitting headache. My tummy felt like a beach ball with four liters of that stuff seemingly stuck in my stomach, yet to work its way down to my colon. Although many patients in Japan choose to have this procedure with no pain medication or anesthesia, my doctor mercifully gave me a sedative through an IV drip which both made me loopy and gave me relief from my headache. Best of all, much to my relief the doctor was able to successfully finish the colonoscopy despite my troubles. Needless to say, this is not something I look forward to going through every two years.

The thing is, my doctor knows I am a freak of nature (he pretty much told me the last time there are few people cursed with such slow-moving bowels!), but he still doesn't come up with any ideas to make the experience more bearable or the test more successful. Even drinking the medication the night before was my idea, not his. I mean, this is a really hard thing for me to go through, and he knows it. Every time I suffer, and every time the medicine doesn't work. I wish he would be more proactive in thinking of a different medication, a different diet, a different course of action. Something. I really like him, and he is a genuinely nice guy. It's funny. After I wrote this chapter, I had my first appointment since my latest colonoscopy torture session. For the first time he actually asked me questions to try to figure out why I have such slow-moving bowels. Do you exercise regularly? Do you usually get constipated? I was happy that he was finally engaging me to try to find answers. That is what I wanted from him all along. I am not expecting him to know all the answers--I just want to believe that he is trying to find them.

There is so much good, so much to be thankful for regarding the medical system in Japan. I am 95% satisfied, and I know that I would probably be much more dissatisfied by the state of things in the U.S. While the 5% dissatisfaction is annoying and frustrating, as with anything, you have to take the good with the bad. The low cost, fairness and accessibility of the medical system outweighs the craziness that is emergency care and weak-kneed doctors, and I would miss the medical care here (and risk personal bankruptcy) if I were ever to go home. In fact, the great social health care system is one of the things we consider most when we talk about returning to the U.S. someday. It is not perfect, but nothing is. Besides, if it were perfect, I wouldn't have as many good stories to tell.

#3

Pregnancy and Childbirth

妊娠
出産

In June of 2009, I found myself relaxing in my luxurious room waiting for the masseuse to come and give me an aromatherapy massage. That night, I was treated to a full-course French meal prepared by a trained chef, including *hors d'oeuvres* and *flambé*. It was the first time in my life I had been pampered so extravagantly. No, I wasn't on vacation at a resort spa. On the contrary, I had just had my third child, and I was in the hospital.

Japanese maternity hospitals are famous for their pampering of new mommies. It seems they are always trying to outdo each other, possibly a tactic to reduce the plummeting birth rate and entice more women to be fruitful and multiply. I personally think it will take more than a few *hors d'oeuvres* to reverse this worsening trend, but, hey, I'm not complaining. They can pamper me all they want.

When I found out I was pregnant for the first time in January of 2005, I wasn't thinking about any of this, though. Five weeks pregnant, I found myself hospitalized in a foreign land with the flu and a flare up of my ulcerative colitis. While neither of these conditions alone was serious enough to require hospitalization, together, along with the risky first few weeks of pregnancy, they were cause for concern. My doctor wanted to hospitalize me as a precaution. While this big university hospital treated me well, I wasn't sure that I wanted to deliver my baby there because I had heard so many good things about private maternity clinics in my city. University hospitals tend to be sterile and impersonal, but are the place to be for high-risk pregnancies. Since my colitis was relatively under control, I decided I would try a local maternity clinic, Angel Hospital, which had a great reputation in my area. If I had any serious complications, I would be sent to the university hospital anyway, so what the heck? I would give it a try.

It didn't start out well. The first time I went, I didn't have an appointment so I had to wait four hours. I thought about throwing in the towel and going somewhere else, but I really liked my doctor, Dr. Yanai, a lot. He was so friendly and down-to-earth. So I decided to think of a strategy where I wouldn't have to wait too long. At that time, there were no appointments for anyone until the final month of pregnancy, so pretty much everyone was in the same boat as I was. It was a first come, first served system. There is no way that everyone else waits four hours every appointment, so I figured there had to be a way around the long waits. I realized that going around lunchtime was the worst plan because you had to wait behind all the people who had been coming all morning. Most Japanese clinics usually have morning slots, take one to three hours off for lunch, then have afternoon slots. Often however, they fall behind schedule, so those with early afternoon appointments have to wait for the doctors to get through the backload of morning appointments before they get to them. However, I figured out that if I were to go around 4:30, right before closing time, the longest I would have to wait was one hour because everyone had to be finished by 5:30, right? So, for the rest of the pregnancy, this was my plan. From that point on, I went for almost all my appointments at 4:30 on Saturday and just like I thought, I never had to wait more than an hour. Like a lot of things in Japan, there is a way around most inconvenience; you just have to figure out what it is.

One awesome thing about pregnancy in Japan is the ultrasound. I should have used the plural there. Ultrasounds. You get an ultrasound every single time you go in to see the doctor. I mean, every single time. I hear in the U.S. most women in normal pregnancies have an ultrasound once when they find out they are pregnant, and once about the midway point. My U.S. friends cannot believe the number of ultrasounds I had. I lost count, but I had to have had at least twenty for each pregnancy. I think I can make a small photo book out of them. I even got an ultrasound when I went in between visits for a cold, even though I had had one only four days earlier. I remember smiling when my American friends talked about how they were so excited to finally get the see their baby on ultrasound, feeling excitement for days, and making sure their husbands were off work so they could hear the baby's heartbeat for the first time. What is considered normal practice here is an event looked forward to for months in the U.S. In case you are wondering if I took these regular ultrasounds for granted, the answer is, not at all. I was moved all sixty or so times I saw my babies on that screen.

I also got videos of every ultrasound, which are among my most treasured possessions. I even got some cool 4D ultrasounds where you can actually see the facial features of the baby in sepia. Of course, there are some drawbacks to having ultrasounds all the time. You tend to worry more when there really is nothing to worry about. For example, through the regular ultrasounds, I found out the umbilical cord was wrapped around both Abby's and Emmy's necks. The doctor wasn't worried about it at all; he told me one-third of babies were born that way, that you should only worry if it was wrapped around the neck 3 or 4 times (which it wasn't). But every time I had an ultrasound, there was no change, so I worried anyway. My third daughter Emmy stopped growing about 35 weeks, so I worried endlessly at the end of that pregnancy. It really wasn't a big deal; she was born a little small but perfectly healthy. However, I would not have worried at all if the doctor had not estimated her weight at every ultrasound. On the other hand, I have friends who have lost babies due to cord accidents because they didn't get regular ultrasounds, so I think the pros of having them actually outweigh the cons. I often wonder if it is the health insurance system in the U.S. that prevents people from having more ultrasounds. It makes me sad because it seems that so many tragedies could be prevented through more regular ultrasound. It cannot be that they are that expensive, because I would just pay a few dollars for one, at 30% out-of-pocket cost.

The cost, or lack thereof, is another plus. From midway through my third pregnancy, all prenatal check-ups in my city became free, which saved us a lot of money. Up to that point, I had always thought that having a baby was cheap in Japan, with the exception of the prenatal checkups, which ran about fifty bucks a pop. That can add up over a nine-month pregnancy. I remember at the end when I was seeing my doctor every week how I would hope I would go into labor before the next checkup to save a few bucks. I may seem like a cheapskate, but 200 bucks a month starts to hurt a little bit. The free checkups really made a difference to me and countless other families in my city.

Of course, all the expensive pre-natal checkups were forgotten due to the low cost of childbirth. When I say low, I mean, low. Like zero. Some people even make a profit on the whole deal.

All new parents pay for the entire cost of labor and childbirth upon discharge from the hospital. At most places you must pay in cash, so everyone has to go to the bank, take out a load of money, and pray they don't get mugged before they get to the hospital. Each city and each hospital has different fees, but when my children were born the going rate in my city was between 350,000 and 450,000 yen (3500-4500 dollars). Then, you go home, fill out the paperwork to get reimbursed (Japanese people love paperwork), and the government, namely the national health care system, would pay you back about a month later. The payout from the government has changed numerous times over the years, so the amount I received was different for all three births. It was between 350,000 and 420,000 yen ($3500-$4200), an amount which covered the entire cost of labor and delivery each time. Of course, the prenatal visits with my first two were costly, but with my third, almost everything was free. I hear that in big cities like Tokyo, some clinics will charge more, 400,000 to 600,000 yen. The payout from the government is uniform throughout the country, so new parents in big cities are probably ending up in the red.

Here's the thing: these fees are more than reasonable even if you don't have health insurance, because in Japan you are in the hospital almost a week after childbirth, eating gourmet food and getting massages. Many American hospitals will charge over six thousand dollars for a problem-free delivery and next-day hospital discharge. Maybe the Japanese pamper new moms a little with the long hospitalization, but why not? I think new moms deserve to be pampered and I milked it for all it was worth (no pun intended!). I have never been able to relate to how American moms can't wait to get out of the hospital and go home. I wanted to stay even longer, the main reason being just to rest. Having a baby is exhausting, and the first three months even worse, so my week in the hospital was kind of like a calm before the storm. The midwife staff would watch the baby at night in the nursery, and call my room when she woke up hungry. I would go to the nursing room, nurse the baby, and go back to sleep.

The hospital offered a 3000 yen (30 dollars) per day discount if new mothers kept the babies with them in their room instead of in the nursery at night. Most moms feel guilty after a night or two, as I did after my first daughter was born, and end up keeping the baby with them. But the second and third time around, my new bundles of joy hung out in the nursery with the midwives the whole week. Yep, call me a bad mom if you want, but I was going to be joined at the boob to the baby for the next year, so I had no guilt at all about keeping her in the nursery so I could get some rest. Not an ounce of guilt. The hospital could gladly keep my 30 bucks. I was getting some sleep.

In addition to wanting rest, I am sure that the yummy food and massages, neither of which is available to U.S. moms, also contributed to my lack of desire to go home. The luxurious pampering of new moms was not just limited to the food and massages. It got even better if you upgraded to the VIP rooms. While it may sound like a resort spa yet again, it was just a normal option given to patients at my clinic.

A regular private room at Angel Hospital had a bed, toilet and sink, and TV, but patients had to go down the hall to use the shower. This basic room was included in the hospitalization fees, so most patients chose to stay here. While the basic rooms were very nice, I decided that I needed a little extra pampering. I chose to pay an extra 5000 yen (50 dollars) a night for an upgrade to a VIP room. It was so awesome that I joyfully and willingly shelled out the extra bucks for my next two pregnancies, too. The rooms were like hotel rooms-soft mattresses with luxurious bedding; private bath and shower; wireless Internet and computer; sofa and chairs. The chef at the French restaurant personally brought me my afternoon snack. I often wondered why all Japanese moms didn't choose this option. My thinking was, "Everything else is free, so why not pay an extra $300 to be pampered and live in luxury for a week?"

My hospital VIP room.

Many of my friends told me that it was too much of a splurge, too expensive. Just like thinking the vaccination for mumps is too expensive, Japanese moms don't know just how ridiculously cheap the pregnancy and childbirth experience is in Japan. Unlike me, they have nothing to compare it to. Sometimes I wish my friends would loosen up a little and splurge on something that happens so infrequently in life. It is like Japanese women feel guilty spending money on themselves, but will gladly spend it on their kids' piano lessons. I often get massages at a local *onsen* to relax, but most of my mommy friends would never even think about splurging like that. So, I sometimes give them gift cards to get free massages as a Christmas present. The key is to give my mommy friends something that they would never buy for themselves.

Anyway, the culture being as it is, most of my friends think it is an unnecessary expense to upgrade to the VIP room. The regular rooms are pretty nice, I admit, but they do not have all the luxuries or a private shower. I joked that since I had my babies too fast to have an epidural, I used the money I saved on a private room. No joke. Epidurals are considered luxuries, too, unnecessary in Japan, so they are not covered by national health care. One epidural will cost about $500 dollars, and even then they just dull the pain. Besides, even if you want one, you are not guaranteed to get it. If you happen to go into labor on a weekend, holiday, or some other time when there is no one qualified to administer an epidural at the hospital, you are out of luck. I am told by my mommy friends that one reason Japanese moms don't get epidurals is because they feel the pain is natural and helps them feel more like they have become mothers, but I wonder if in the back of their minds, they are also thinking about the cost. There is a proverb in Japan that having a baby is like pushing a watermelon through your nose. Even that kind of pain is not enough to get women to ask for an epidural like western women. The wimpy American in me doesn't understand the necessity of this sacrifice. I haven't decided yet if I think Japanese mommies are courageous or crazy.

In addition to the other luxuries, every Tuesday and Friday we would get a full-course French meal. My third pregnancy, I lucked out with the timing and I was hospitalized from Monday to Saturday, so I was there for two meals. Patients can choose to eat in their rooms, or in the dining room with the other patients. Of course, if you eat in your room, you cannot experience the flambé or other tricks the chef does. While eating, patients talk about their pregnancy and childbirth journey with other patients, doctors and midwives. It is so encouraging and moving to hear the stories of the other mommies. Unfortunately for me, I dislike French food, so I often traded my husband for a convenience store beef bowl. My friends crack up at that one. It is like trading a steak for a McDonalds hamburger.

The luxuries are the main thing many people here focus on, but not me. For me, the absolutely best thing about having a baby in Japan was the kindness of everyone involved in the experience. The doctors, nurses, midwives—everyone was wonderful and contributed to my amazing childbirth experiences in Japan. I received unbelievable compassion and care from these people. I don't cry much (except when watching *Steel Magnolias*--I always bawl at that one!) but I was so moved by the love and compassion of the staff at my hospital that I cried when I was discharged after the birth of my first daughter Mia. Of course, the hormones were probably also partly to blame, but I was so nervous having a baby in a foreign country, and they made me feel so loved. I remember one of the midwives said to me, "I know that your family is not here, so please think of us as your Japanese family. We are here for you." They meant it. They have been treating me like family ever since.

There was a 24-hour nursing room in the hospital staffed by midwives for those new mothers who needed help with nursing. In Japan, midwives work together alongside doctors in maternity hospitals. They first get regular nursing degrees, and then two extra years of training to become midwives. They are very much in the mainstream in the Japanese medical community. Generally, nurses will help the doctors with prenatal checkups, and midwives will work in the delivery ward helping deliver babies and give advice about breastfeeding.

Breastfeeding is encouraged in Japan, and the rate of breastfeeding is much higher than in America. Of course, many women will use formula if they are unable to nurse, but most women here desire to try breastfeeding, at least for a while. It is such a normal topic of conversation here, that I was shocked at first at how naturally this topic came up in daily life. One day, this stranger came up to me and said, "Oh my goodness! Your baby is so cute! Are you producing a lot of milk?" I stumbled, "Uh, yeah, sure, a pretty normal amount, I guess." Japanese kids are always talking about their mommy's *oppai* (boobs). There are children's songs praising the *oppai*. The lyrics go something like, "*Mommy's boobs are so full of milk! They are soft. I really want to drink it...Yeah!*" Once, at a winter recital at my kids's preschool, one class did a little play about how much each of them loved their mommy's *oppai* and why. The milk is yummy. The boobs are soft. I am not kidding. Luckily, my daughters' classes haven't done that one yet, so I have escaped the world knowing the wonders of my *oppai*. But Emmy still has three years left at preschool, meaning three winter recitals, so I am not out of the woods yet.

Depending on context, *oppai* can actually mean breast, breastfeeding, or breast milk. It is a very versatile word. For the postpartum new mommy in Japan, breastfeeding is probably the number one source of both joy and anxiety, and I wasn't any different. I really appreciated the nursing room at the hospital because I had a lot of nursing problems with my first daughter, Mia (I was a pro after that, so they pretty much ignored me!). One midwife in particular stayed by my side almost all day giving me advice about nursing my baby, giving me the most painful breast massage of my life, and just generally supporting me. This midwife, Ikue, is like family to us now, as is Dr. Yanai, who delivered all three of my girls. We love him like family. He gave us so much love and support during the pregnancies, and I know that I can trust him no matter what. While most patients cannot be sure if their favorite doctor will be available when they go into labor, I knew that Dr. Yanai would come to deliver my kids no matter what time it was or what he was doing. And he did.

I was a little ticked off at him while I was in labor with Emmy, though. He had been saying the whole pregnancy how when contractions finally came, she would be born quickly. She dropped early, and was low for much of the last trimester. Because Abby had been born so quickly, in less than two hours, I naively assumed that Emmy would be the quickest and easiest of all. Boy was I wrong. Because I was induced due to IUGR (Intrauterine Growth Retardation) nothing about my labor proceeded naturally, including the pace. The contractions were so painful so early on in the labor, and after a while I stopped progressing at all. I still remember how discouraging it was when after enduring a hard hour of labor, the midwives found that I had not progressed at all. This was turning into the most painful one yet. When Dr. Yanai came in to see how I was doing, I yelled at him for lying to me and lulling me in to assuming I was in for a walk in the park, when in reality it felt like the New York City Marathon. I got revenge on him by peeing on him. Really. I actually peed on him when I got to the pushing part. I know that many people, including me, get an enema because whatever is in you is gonna come out with the baby. Most people don't want to be embarrassed by that, so they just get the enema beforehand to guard against it. You cannot do anything about pee, though, and I sprayed him good. Of course, I later apologized about yelling at him, but not about the pee. He was very forgiving, of course. You cannot hold a pregnant woman responsible for anything she says or does during childbirth.

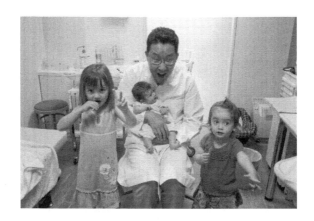

Dr. Yanai delivered all three of our girls.

I have a very special relationship to this day with Angel Hospital. For two years, I taught English to the midwives because of the increase in foreign patients choosing to give birth at Angel. They needed to know how to say a little more than "Don't push!" We developed a bond through that, and now, even though I do not teach that class anymore, I still see them regularly. When Emmy, my youngest, was born, the labor room was full with midwife friends who came to check on me even though they were not on duty. Ikue was so committed to our family that we picked her up on the way to the hospital. She wanted to deliver my baby herself even though she had just finished a night shift and was sleepless and exhausted. Luckily, the labor progressed slowly so she could get come sleep.

Dr. Yanai and I also communicate often. I know if I ever need anything, I can ask, and he will help me no matter what. Sometimes, it is sad because since it has been three years since my last child was born, there is no reason for me to go to the hospital anymore. I don't get to see my friends as much as I used to, and this is hard for me. Riz and I would love to have another baby (maybe a boy?) to add to our family. I often joke with my friends at Angel that I am going to have to get pregnant again just to see them more. Of course this is not the reason we want to get pregnant, but getting to see them again on a regular basis is just an extra perk. These people truly are my Japanese family, and I know that my experience with pregnancy and childbirth would not have been nearly as wonderful if I had not chosen this hospital. I am sure that there are many similar places in Japan with luxurious rooms, food, and services. But as great as that was, that is not what moved me. It was the love and compassion the staff had for me. If I had to choose between the people and the stuff, I would choose the people every time. I have no regrets about having babies in Japan, not even the pain, because it was everything together that made it such a wonderful experience. I never want to have a baby anywhere else.

My midwife buddies at the birth of my third child, Emmy.

Finally, I wanted to sing the praises of the *boshi techo*. This is literally translated "Maternal and Child Health Handbook." Around 12 weeks of pregnancy, all expectant mothers go to the local ward office to pick up this treasure. From this point on, until your kid is 18, this is ultimate growth chart/all-inclusive record of everything. Japanese obstetricians record all pregnancy data in this little book: mother's weight gain, baby's growth, blood work, ultrasounds, and fetal position. Every number from every doctor's visit is recorded in this book. When it is time to deliver the baby, detailed information about the birth is also recorded: the baby's size, labor time, complications, *Apgar* Score, method of delivery. Comments from the doctor and midwives are even included. This little book is awesome because the mothers and fathers will be able to refer to it later when reflecting on the birth, or they can use it to compare the pregnancies and deliveries of subsequent children.

After birth, the *boshi techo* records Mom's postpartum physical and emotional state, weight loss (hopefully not the other way around!), and the baby's growth and immunization record. My hospital has free weight checks (for the baby) and nursing consultation for mothers after they are discharged. They check the baby's weight before and after nursing to see how much milk he is getting. This is a big comfort, because all new nursing moms know the anxiety of having no idea how much milk the baby is getting in the early days. After Mia was born, we actually rented a baby scale for a month. Formula-fed babies and their moms don't have to deal with this anxiety, but of course, they are welcome to the weigh-ins too. The results of the weigh-ins, along with a note of encouragement, are recorded in the *boshi techo.* The notes of from the midwives are awesome; "Mia is a drinking machine! She is a pro, and will grow in no time!" In all my pregnancies, especially the first one, these free consultations eased my mind, and also gave me an excuse to go to the hospital and see my buddies again.

The all-important boshi techo: maternal and child health handbook.

Probably the most important record is of childhood immunizations and illnesses. All immunizations, and many illnesses, are recorded here. After I first learned about the *boshi techo,* I often wondered why Americans don't use something similar. I mean, I know my mom had no idea what immunizations I had gotten, and that was with us living in the same house my entire childhood. What do families do that move all the time? I am sure Mom had to call our doctor's office to check when immunization information was needed. Sometimes a mother's sketchy knowledge is not enough, with schools and employers requiring proof at times. What a complicated mess. The *boshi techo* solves all of this. Unless of course, you lose it, in which case it becomes a huge headache and hassle. There are few things in my possession that I would rather not lose than my girls' *boshi techos.* I think it would be more inconvenient than losing their passports.

It is so practical, but so fun at the same time. In Japan, babies have a 3-month, 1 1/2 year, and 3-year check-up to measure growth, which of course is all recorded in the *boshi techo.* It is fun to compare the growth and development of my three kids. It is also interesting to see how my weight gain varied from child to child. I gained a lot more with my first child than with the other three, but for all of them, most of the weight gain happened in the middle. I remember gaining eight pounds one month and being annoyed because I didn't feel like I was eating any more than usual. But I just looked at my *boshi techo* and realized this happened all three times, so I am pretty sure that is just the way my body works. Yep, right there. Weeks 15-20 are very, very dangerous.

The Japanese are obsessive about weight gain during pregnancy. Like crazy, psycho, wacked out. Crazy. Without fail, the second question asked when you meet a friend (the first being, "Is the baby doing okay?") is "How much weight have you gained?" The Japanese standard for weight gain during pregnancy is about 7-10 kilograms (15-22 pounds), but most say that an eight-kilogram (17.6 pounds) weight gain is best. The U.S. OB/GYN association recommends 25-35 pounds (11-16 kilograms) for normal weight women. This is a pretty big difference. Most Japanese women I know are really careful with their weight, some to the point of even dieting during pregnancy. Everyone knows this is crazy due to the extra nutrition pregnant women need to take care of the growing fetus. I gained twelve kilograms with my first child, and seven with my second and third. All the kids were born at a normal size, but my third was a little small (about 6 pounds) for a full-term baby by U.S. standards. I do think the U.S. standard is a little too high and that there is no way you need an extra 35 pounds during pregnancy.

That said, the Japanese obsession about weight gain is more than a little disturbing to me. One of my friends was told that she was not allowed to gain more than eight kilograms during her entire pregnancy, or more than 1.5 kilograms per month. If she did, it showed a lack of self-control and that hospital would kick her out. They wouldn't see her anymore. She was ordered to weigh herself three times a day. It is a wonder that Japanese women don't develop eating disorders during pregnancy; in fact, who knows, maybe they do.

Angel Hospital is very laid back about weight gain. They have a general recommendation, 7-12 kilograms, but if mother and child are healthy, they don't really say anything. This is how it should be. One of my midwife friends there is a legend. She is pregnant again, and has at least a 20 kg (44 pounds) weight gain with every pregnancy. They all wonder if she is a going for her personal best with this one. She is healthy and so is the baby, and she always loses it after childbirth. I never felt pressured by the doctors or staff about my weight, and I appreciated that. But still, I became so self-conscious about weight gain that I found myself not eating before my check-ups because I was afraid of gaining those extra grams before the appointment. After all, my weight would be recorded in my *boshi techo*, never to be erased, available for anyone to see at anytime for all eternity. I wish I could write here that I resisted the cultural pressure to be obsessed with weight, that I cared only for the baby, but I can't. I, too, obsessed about not only the weight gain, but also about losing it after childbirth. I couldn't wait to get back to the gym. Unfortunately, nursing didn't melt away the pounds for me after childbirth. Nope. It was Billy Blanks' Boot Camp and Jillian's 30-Day Shred. Good, old-fashioned hard work and sweat. I wanted to punch my metabolically-blessed friends who said, "Oh my. I am eating like a pig everyday and I am still losing weight like crazy!" Growl. Hiss. Boo! Most Japanese women are back in their skinny jeans faster than you can say apple pie, which is what they eat everyday and still lose their baby weight in about a month.

So, while having my children in Japan was one of the best experiences of my life, looking back I think pregnancy and childbirth also contributed to my sliding back into the eating disorder that I thought I had overcome in college. But really, do you ever really overcome an eating disorder? When I was in the eighth grade, my basketball coach told me that I would be a better player if I lost some weight. At that time, I was 5 foot 7 and 165 pounds. Although others had told me the same thing my whole life, for some reason hearing it from my coach was different. I immediately went on a diet, and lost forty pounds in four months or so. I guess that was a little extreme, but it would have been fine had it stopped there. But my thirteen-year-old psyche was damaged forever by all the new friends I had, and by my newfound popularity. People suddenly liked me a lot more, and I knew that if I got fat again that would change. I decided I needed to lose more weight and stopped eating breakfast and lunch, even though I was practicing every afternoon with the basketball team. For dinner I would eat a head of cabbage (yes, a head) or a Weight Watchers frozen dinner, and then do the same thing the next day. And the next. I remember once my friends holding me down in the cafeteria trying to make me eat. But it didn't work because I didn't think I had a problem. All I knew was that food was the enemy now, the thing that would keep me from the friends and popularity I so desperately craved.

In college it got so bad that my dorm mates told my RA she needed to talk to me. I saw a counselor who didn't help at all, but what did help was my newfound Christian faith. I am convinced that coming to faith in Christ that year saved my life, and helped me to see that I am loved for who I am and not for how much I weigh. I sometimes wonder if I would have killed myself from lack of food had I not become a Christian. And while I never forced myself to throw up or anything, I would excessively exercise if I felt guilty about eating something, which was pretty much all the time. Three hours at the gym would take away the guilt of too many cookies or too much hot chocolate, both of which I loved. I know it is hard for people who have never struggled with an eating disorder to understand, but the feeling of being full always led to guilt, even if it was a tummy full of veggies.

After my freshman year, my thoughts turned to my new Christian life, my new love of academics and my passion for being a religion major. I loved studying religion, even though I was at a secular college and my faith was often challenged by my non-religious professors. My eating struggles all but disappeared, and I actually gained 20 pounds or so by graduation, and stayed there throughout my grad school days, early married life, and my first stint in Japan. I was a little overweight, but okay with that, and I did not think about it all that much.

I really think that it was pregnancy and childbirth that triggered a relapse for me into unhealthy eating habits and negative thoughts about food. I gained so much weight with Mia during my first pregnancy. Even after she was born, I still had so much flab. I remember the thing that motivated me to join the gym. Mia was about four months old, just started to stand a little. She was jumping up and down on my tummy, and sinking pretty deeply into the layers of flab. Nope, I didn't like this. This flab had to go. After joining the gym, I lost most of the baby weight and more, getting down to my pre-pregnancy weight of 66 kg (145 pounds), and more, leveling off at 58 kg (126 pounds). I looked and felt great, and was not that screwed up about food.

But after Abby and Emmy were born, I got obsessive about diet and exercise, sometimes waking up at 3 am and working out three hours a day. I ate less than a normal person and exercised more, getting down to 54 kg (119 pounds), which I delusionally thought was my ideal weight. I wouldn't call it anorexia or bulimia, just a generally unhealthy view of food and of myself. After I stopped nursing Emmy, I still didn't get my period back, so I went back to Angel Hospital. I wanted to have another baby, and I needed a period for that to be possible. My doctor gave me medicine to start my cycle, and while I did menstruate, as soon as I stopped taking the medicine, my period would stop again. Nothing seemed to work, and after a while I stopped thinking about having another baby; I just wanted to be normal and healthy.

My doctor didn't think it had anything to do with my weight, and maybe it didn't, but it was definitely related to my exercise obsession. I know it. I didn't want to admit it, but it had to be true. There was really no other explanation that I could think of. The medication just made me gain weight and grumpy, which made things worse, so I stopped taking it. I hated how it made me feel. It was the end of January, and I decided that if I didn't get my period back by the end of February, I would go back to the doctor and resume the medication. I prayed to God that this wouldn't have to happen. Then, on February 29 (it was a leap year), I got my period, without medication, for the first time in almost three years. God really does answer prayer in His own time. Prayer, my own and that of my family and friends, helped me get back on a healthier path. I started eating more and exercising less, and my period started coming every now and then. Not as regular as I would like, but I'll take it.

I wish I could say now that I am healed, but I have come to realize that an eating disorder is not unlike alcoholism and drug addiction. You are never really healed of it. It is always there, lurking under the surface of my emotions, ready to jump out anytime there is a weak spot in my heart. I hate it and I hate that I struggle with it. I sometimes look at skinny people and hate them for being able to eat whatever they want to and not get fat. I start to feel sorry for myself. Why do I have to have such a slow metabolism? Why do I have ulcerative colitis, which dictates what I can and cannot eat? Why do I have an eating disorder? Seems unfair to me sometimes that I have so many different food issues to deal with. (Did I mention my hereditary high cholesterol that keeps me away from too many eggs, one of my favorite foods?) But this self-pity doesn't last too long. I realize that those skinny people have other issues they are dealing with that I have no idea about. Maybe they are addicted to drugs or smoking. Maybe they are in unhappy marriages or an abusive situation. Maybe they are struggling with depression. Maybe they are just lonely. I don't know. I do know that we all have issues, and that nobody is perfect. We all have struggles, and the struggles that skinny people have are just as hard for them to deal with as my issues with food. I don't really know why I have this burden that seems to weigh me down and crush me at times, but I do believe with all that is within me that everything happens for a reason, even if I cannot see it now. Maybe one day I will be able to help someone struggling with food issues because of what I have gone through and am going through still. My goal now is only to eat well one day at a time, and to know that, fat or skinny, weak or strong, God loves me. And that is enough to get me through any day.

Pregnant with my third child.

Sometimes I do wonder if I should leave this country of skinny people and go back to the U.S., a place where I would be the skinny person. Maybe the temptation to not eat enough and compare myself to others would be lessened. But maybe if I did that, I would not rely on God as much as I need to, maybe it would be taking the easy way out when in reality, God wants me to grow through my struggles and come to a place of freedom. A place where I come to accept that my body will never be as it was before having kids and the stretched-out skin on my tummy will never disappear. A place where I am 100% okay with that. Maybe I am not there yet, but my three beautiful daughters are worth all the eating struggles, all the stretch marks, all the saddlebags in the world. And I wouldn't trade them for anything.

#4

Japanese People

日本人

I remember that day like it was yesterday, even though it was almost fifteen years ago. It was the fall of 1997, and I had just arrived in Japan. I had been looking for an English-teaching job in the Kansai area, but had not had any luck. I was tired and frustrated, because I had mistakenly believed that I would have no trouble finding a job since I was a native English speaker. I soon learned that employers greatly preferred applicants with what the newspaper called a "proper visa," meaning that you already have some kind of working visa or permission from the government to work. I had neither, and if I was going to work, I needed a working visa from my employer. Nationals of Canada, New Zealand, England, and Australia had an advantage over me as an American —they could enter under the working holiday system, meaning they had a "proper visa" and could get hired much more easily than I could. I learned that America is the only major native English-speaking country that does not have this mutual cultural exchange system with Japan in place. The paperwork and responsibilities involved in getting a working visa for employees is a major headache, and employers much prefer hiring people who already have one. Finding a job was much harder than I had expected, and I was wondering if I should just take whatever job I could find.

I was in Osaka one day looking for the place where I was to interview for a full-time position at an English conversation school. In the 80s, these jobs were easy to get and paid great. However, with the bursting of the bubble, the depreciation of the yen, and the increase of foreigners into Japan, it became harder to get a job, especially for those without the "proper visa." At that time, I had just come to Japan and my Japanese was terrible. It consisted mainly of greetings and survival Japanese. I could not find the place I was supposed to be. Japanese streets, for the most part, do not have names. There are blocks, and while it may make some sense to the initiated, to the uninitiated, it is a maze of confusion like, "Turn left at the temple, walk two streets and turn right at a long row of vending machines. Look for the house with the dog and turn right. My house is the one with the tin roof and red car in front." Now, of course, with GPS, navigating is much easier, but at that time it was a mess, especially for a *gaijin* (foreigner) who couldn't communicate a lick.

So here I am looking for the conversation school, but I could not find it and had no idea how to look. I looked around for a friendly-looking face, found one, and asked for help. I showed this nice middle-aged lady my map in Japanese and added my broken Japanese for good measure. This lady not only told me where to go, but she personally took me there. And I do not remember it being all that close, either. Perhaps she took me because it was easier to just show me than to try to explain in Japanese or worse, English. However, I prefer to think that is was a prime example of the Japanese spirit of hospitality, the willingness to go out of their way to help others, especially a helpless, pitiful *gaijin* like me. Of course, for every nice lady to help the *gaijin*, there is another Japanese who will run screaming in the other direction, "I don't speak English!!" (even if you ask in Japanese). I remember the time in Kobe I asked a man for directions to Sannomiya Station in perfect Japanese. With a terrified look on his face the man gestured while shouting, "Straight! Straight! Straight!" It turned out, it wasn't straight. That being said, most Japanese people will go out of their way time and time again to help others. I have experienced this kindness more times than I can count.

Most people who have ever lived in Japan will tell you that the Japanese people are the nicest in the world, and they will do anything for you. I can tell you after 13 years here that this is true. It takes so long to really get to know people, and if you think Japanese are helpful to strangers, you should see how they treat family and friends. Sometimes I have to be careful to not tell someone I like something too much out of fear that they may give it to me. Once my mom told a friend that she was looking for some wallets made from traditional Japanese cloth; my friend promptly went out and bought two of them—exactly what my mom wanted, and would accept no money from my mom in return.

Sometimes, though, the gift giving can get a little out of control. One example is the Japanese custom of buying souvenirs, or *omiyage*.. Every time someone goes anywhere, there is a cultural obligation to buy *omiyage* of that place (most commonly a snack or some kind of sweets) for everybody from your boss to your friends to your fourth cousin twice removed. Maybe that is a little hyperbole, but they do buy way more gifts for friends and colleagues than Americans do. Long ago I got tired of trying to keep up with it all, so now I just buy gifts for close friends. And yes, I am sure that I am not the only one who keeps a trip a secret sometimes so no *omiyage* is expected on my return.

When this gift-giving obsession meets the Japanese concept of duty the result is the *okaeshi*. This is a complicated beast, but as I understand it, when someone gives you a gift, you are obligated to return the favor. Of course, this is not set in stone, but for a big life event like the birth of a baby, most gifts are acknowledged with an official return gift. The most common *okaeshi* for baby gifts is some kind of food or drink with the child's name written elaborately in Japanese calligraphy on a paper attached to the gift. The return gift must be between one-third and one-half of the value of the original gift. I don't know how anyone finds time for this complicated process during the months after having a baby.

For weddings, since guests are expected to give a monetary gift of $300 (single) or $500 (couple), the *okaeshi is* a lot more extravagant, usually expensive dishes or foods. And no, that amount is not a typo. Guests are for the most part paying for their own zillion course French meal, and helping to pay for the wedding, which will run between $30,000 and $50,000. My husband and I have twice spent almost $1500 to attend a wedding when travel costs, hotel and gifts are all added together. The bride and groom will chip in a little to help out, but you still end up in a considerable financial hole. Makes you not want to get invited to a wedding, doesn't it? But alas, this chapter is about the blessing that Japanese people are to us, and of course, we would not have gone to the weddings in the first place if the people getting married hadn't been so special to us. Some missionary friends of ours were on such a tight budget that they instituted a no-wedding policy. They figured it was the only way to financially survive in Japan.

The thing that I don't like about the *okaeshi* system is that I just want to give a gift with no strings attached. I am not expecting anything back, and I don't want anything back. I just want that person to know that I am thinking about them and they matter to me. But even when I just make brownies or cookies for someone, the Tupperware always comes back with some candies or snacks inside. It is never anything big or expensive, of course, but always something. My friend, who is British, told me his Japanese wife just can't bring herself to give back an empty Tupperware. He has no trouble, though. He once ate twelve of my brownies in an hour, and then gave me back an empty Tupperware without even washing it. Maybe it's not the best manners in the world, but part of me prefers his way. The fact that he couldn't stop himself from consuming 2000 sugary calories in an hour was proof enough they were good, and his simple thank you was the kind of *okaeshi* I like best.

I finally stumbled on a way to not get a Tupperware back full of goodies. Recently, I have begun giving baked goodies in disposable containers, like boxes or trays. When I do this, I never get an *okaeshi* back. Eureka! I have found it! I am baking brownies for friends because I love them, and the last thing I want to do is burden them with the responsibility of giving me *okaeshi*. Sometimes I think maybe it is best not to give them anything; then they won't feel obligated to return the favor. What if my intended blessing is actually a curse? Even if I tell someone they don't have to return the favor, they usually do anyway because their culture demands it, and it is ingrained in them from birth. I love baking, I love my friends, and I love giving gifts, so for now I'll just keep trekking to the local 100 yen shop for more disposable plastic trays.

My favorite okaeshi: a set of Winnie the Pooh dishes received at a friend's wedding.

There are times when the Japanese are not always so friendly. There is a concept in Japan called *uchi* (inside) and *soto* (outside). The *uchi* is the group of friends and family around a person. The *soto* is everybody else. Japanese people will do anything for the people in their *uchi*, but tend to often be a little more distant to people in the *soto*. Of course, Japanese are always courteous, and try to avoid bad manners and rudeness at all costs. If asked for help, they will respond with kindness, sometimes to the extent I experienced when looking for my job interview in Osaka. But more often than not, they will try to avoid interaction with the *soto*. This can be seen on trains. Very rarely will people start up conversations with strangers, and eye contact is rare. Most people listen to music, or read comics or newspapers. In the U.S. we often make small talk with strangers on the bus, train, or in stores, but most Japanese just don't make it a habit to talk to strangers.

However, if they see someone often enough, they may start up a conversation after a while. I visit a local bakery every morning for coffee, and there are a handful of other regular customers like me who probably spend hundreds of dollars a month there (okay, maybe only $100). The other regulars are very friendly and we always great each other with "good morning" when we meet, and sometimes will strike up a conversation. This usually happens after seeing each other at the bakery every day for quite a while, so I guess we are not really strangers anymore. It is almost like we have formed our own *uchi* in the bakery, and it is a highlight of my day.

When it comes to the treatment of foreigners, generally people who love English and international things will go out of their way to help them, but others who don't will avoid them like the plague. Someone once said that foreigners, no matter now fluent in Japanese or knowledgeable about Japan, will never be accepted into the *uchi* of Japanese society. They will always be *soto*. Once foreigners accept this fact, they can be happy here. Many foreigners who are unhappy here are the ones who are always trying to get Japan to accept them, to treat them the same as the Japanese. They will not be happy, because this will never happen. We will never be in the *uchi* in Japanese society, but that is okay.

I have been here 13 years, I am fluent in Japanese, and I have no struggles in daily life. But just last year, I was at a hospital for a health checkup, and the nurse called ahead and said, "Now I am bringing Mrs. Tanaka, Mrs. Takahashi, and the foreigner." I was separated, set apart, not allowed into the *uchi*. I don't think the Japanese are being spiteful or trying to discriminate. I just think they do not have a lot of experience with foreigners and are not quite sure yet just what to do with us. There is not even a uniform system in the country for writing our names. There are four alphabets used in Japan--Chinese *kanji* characters are used for Japanese names; *katakana* is used for foreign names; *hiragana*, a phonetic alphabet, is sometimes used for Japanese names, especially by children who cannot yet read *kanji*; and the Roman alphabet. Most of my credit cards, IDs, bankbooks, bills and official documents in Japan have my name written in different ways. Here are some examples:

CRESCINI ANNE MARIE

アン　クレシーニ (an kureshini)

クレシーニ　アン (kureshini an)

ANNEMARIE CRESCINI

Because there is no uniform way to write foreign names in Japan, I have had many headaches, once being denied a credit card because I wrote my name in the wrong alphabet in the wrong order. I have been asked more times than I can remember to make a correction to a form I have already filled out, to write my name in a different way. This happened recently on an application for life insurance. Like I said, I think there is no ill will, just a lack of experience. Of course, Japan is changing, and the number of foreigners has been increasing recently, but it still has a ways to go. As a white American educator, my status here is high and I am treated well, but I often hear that East and South Asians are not given the same respect or treated as well. I am writing about my mostly positive experiences of being treated well, but I am aware that not all foreigners have received such a favorable reception from Japanese society.

One thing that has made my life here so fulfilling is this: I have accepted, even embraced, the fact that I will always be *soto* in Japanese society. I am able to do this because I know I have been accepted into the *uchi* of my particular group of friends, being treated as family by them. This is much more important to me than being in the *uchi* of Japanese society. My husband and I are Christians, have been since college, and this is a very important part of our lives and defines who we are. Upon arriving in Kitakyushu ten years ago, we began looking for a church. Amazingly, we settled on the first one we visited, a small 35-member church called Kitakyushu Bible Church. That church is our family, and we are in the *uchi* there. To illustrate just how wonderful Japanese people are, I just have to talk about one special church member, Junko Fukuda.

Junko and her son, Akira, visiting my family in Virginia during the 2009 Christmas holidays.

I have known Junko since I first arrived at the church. She cracks me up every time she opens her mouth, which is pretty often. She is loud and opinionated--pretty much the opposite of your typical Japanese. She will probably hit me when she reads the part about her being loud and opinionated, but that is why I love her. She has something to say about everything. She is a wonderful cook. Everything she makes is gold, whether meals or desserts, and she can whip up a feast in twenty minutes. I have never seen anything like it. Most Japanese are humble when they present food to others, saying, "Sorry, it tastes so bad, but here you go." Not Junko. She always introduces her culinary creations with, "I don' t wanna be prideful, but this is really awesome!" On the rare occasion she admits failure on a dish, I taste it, and of course, it is awesome, too. I always tell her that her failure tastes better than my success, and I mean it.

Junko is always smiling, always laughing, always making everyone feel right at home. Everyone she meets loves her. But the thing I respect most about her is the love she has for her kids and vice versa. Many young people either don't like their parents or are embarrassed by them. Others love their parents and are thankful for them, but are not that close to them. I can honestly say that Junko's three adult sons absolutely adore their mother and she adores them. They are friends and they love spending time together. They are wonderful members of society, well mannered, and kind, and they love their mommy.

Junko is also a servant. She spends every Thursday preparing desserts for our church's weekly café, and Fridays working all day at the café as a volunteer. She gives so much time and love to the church and people there. She prays without ceasing for everyone in her life, and is always on the lookout to meet a need. She has probably made my family at least thirty meals when we were sick, tired, busy, or just because she loves us.

As I said, Junko is very opinionated and strong-willed, as am I, so there is never a dull moment with us. We argue like cats and dogs sometimes, both being fully convinced that we are right about something. People at church sometimes tell us to calm down and stop fighting, but we know that we are not really fighting, just getting under each other's skin on purpose, and we love every minute of it. Neither of us doubts the love or respect we have for each other. When she does or says something she shouldn't have, I will tell her; likewise, she is one of the only people I know who will tell me when I make a language or cultural mistake. Because I am fluent in Japanese, very few people will correct me when I make a mistake because they always understand what I want to say. But this language is brutal, I am not perfect, and the nuances and cultural connotations are endless. Once, I was using a form of request, which I thought was fine, but Junko told me that it sounded bossy, even if I was addressing someone I was close to. Well, of course, the last thing I wanted was for someone to think I was bossy, so I am glad she loved me enough to tell me.

My Japanese is good, but sometimes I make hilarious goofs. Once I wanted to tell Junko that she was priceless, but I ended up saying she was worthless. Another time, I wanted to say that the local bakery's coffee was a little better than the coffee at the church café, but I ended up saying the equivalent of "the bakery's coffee is the best in the world and the café's coffee tastes like pee."

Like I said, Junko is a prayer warrior. She told me from the moment she met me that she was praying for my husband Riz and I to get pregnant. We had been married for six years, and had decided to put off having kids until we had done some serious traveling and paid back the $35,000 in school loans that were an albatross around our necks. In January of 2005, I came down with what I was sure was the flu. Around the same time, I was having a flare up of my ulcerative colitis. On top of everything, my period was late and I was wondering if I might be pregnant. The previous year, with our loans almost paid off and our travel itch sufficiently scratched, we decided to try to start a family. I stopped taking the pill in September 2004, but I was worried that I would have a hard time getting pregnant. The eating disorder I struggled with in high school had caused me to not have my period for over a year. What if I had messed up my reproductive system in some way? Also, what if taking the pill for so long had made it harder to get pregnant? I was full of worries, but decided there was nothing I could do now but trust God. I was 30, and Riz was 34, and we thought it was the perfect timing for us to have a baby.

When I told my doctor about my flu-like symptoms, colitis flare up and possible pregnancy, he recommended that I be hospitalized immediately as a precaution. If I was pregnant, the other complications could harm the baby in the fragile period of early pregnancy. I freaked out. I wasn't expecting to be told this when I came in for my regular appointment. I called Junko sobbing hysterically. Unfortunately, she had no idea what was wrong with me because she couldn't understand my sobbing, hysterical, accented Japanese, but I managed to get out that I was going to be hospitalized and the name of the hospital, so she came immediately to support me.

I was given a pregnancy test and put in a ward with four other people. I later had to move to a private room since the flu was contagious. It irked me that the cheap private rooms, which were covered by insurance, were full so my only choice was the VIP room, which cost 12,000 yen ($120) a night. Of course, if I didn't want to pay, my other choice was to go home and rest, which was not recommended since it would harm the baby if I were pregnant. Gee, thanks for all the options, doc. I ended up in the VIP room.

After Junko arrived, the doctor came to tell me that I did have the flu, and I was indeed pregnant. The only problem was I did not understand the Japanese word for a positive test result, so I just sat there and smiled. The doctor was speaking in such a monotone, plain voice, that she might as well had said, "Yes, and they are calling for rain tomorrow morning." So, I figured I couldn't be pregnant. That is good news, after all. After the doctor left, I asked Junko what she had said, and she said, "You are pregnant, *jyan!*" Due to my insufficient vocabulary, she found out I was pregnant before I did.

Whether you understand Japanese or not, you will enjoy the background story to the word *jyan*. This is a sentence-ending particle used in northern Japan for emphasis. People in the Kansai and Kyushu areas of Japan don't use it. When I was in graduate school in Virginia, I met a student from Sendai, in Northern Japan. She seemed to put *jyan* on the end of everything, so I started making fun of her by saying stuff that made no sense like, "Hello *jyan.*" "I'm hungry *jyan*," "That's great *jyan*." I would put it in totally nonsensical places when speaking both Japanese and English, just as a joke. I made friends with a group of students from Osaka who were studying at my university, and my crazy *jyan* usage rubbed off on them. Before I knew it, I had created a *jyan* revolution and every Japanese student I knew was using *jyan* in totally inappropriate ways like I was. It was hilarious. We were using *jyan* so much that we couldn't help it. My friends from Kansai were laughed at when they went back to Japan for using *jyan* like that, but they couldn't stop. When I came to Kyushu, my *jyan* revolution spread, and many of my friends at church became crazy *jyan* users, too. Junko is the worst offender, and she is a hoot. When people who Junko has never met come to café for the first time, and she will just burst out, "Hello *jyan*!" or "Welcome to our church, *jyan*!" Never mind that these people can't speak English, let alone understand why she would stick *jyan* on the end of an English sentence. I love this about her. She is absolutely crazy and totally comfortable with who she is. She doesn't care what people think about her. This is really rare in Japan, where conformity to the norm is one of the most important concepts in the culture.

There is a Japanese proverb that says, *"Deru kugi wa utareru"* (The nail that sticks out will be hammered down). This is true. People try really hard not to be different. I even see this in my own kids, who, try as the may, cannot help but be different and stick out. They are light-skinned, round-eyed, half-Caucasian, half-Filipino brunette beauties. They look amazingly like each other and amazingly nothing like me or my husband. They were born in Japan so they are greatly influenced by Japanese culture, yet they are American and we teach them Christian values at home. My oldest, Mia, really hates sticking out. I guess she figures since she sticks out so much already, she wants to keep unnecessary sticking out to a minimum. When she had her elementary school orientation last year, I caught her trying to hide her brown hair under her hat because she didn't want to be different.

Junko sticks out, and she is okay with that. That is why I love her. Her smile and laughter are contagious and everyone who comes into contact with her loves her. I love her like my own mother. While she constantly reminds me she is not old enough to be my mom (she is only 15 years older than I am), sometimes I feel like she is. We laugh and fight and love like mother and daughter, and she is always there for me. Throughout my pregnancy, she was by my side. Since I had never had a baby in Japan (or anywhere else for that matter!) I was really nervous about it. She came with me to my first prenatal checkup, waiting with me four hours before we were finally called in. She took care of me, cooked for me, prayed for me, hung out with me. When it came time for Mia to be born, I insisted that she be in the delivery room with me. I was worried about the language barrier, because at that time I was not as fluent as I am now, especially with the vocabulary. More than anything, though, I just wanted the comfort of her presence. It was a brutal labor, but she was beside me massaging my back the whole time. When Mia was finally born, she was the first one to hold her. When Abby and Emmy were born, I wanted her there, too. Not because of the communication problems, but because of the comfort of her just being there. Except, of course, for the time I wanted to punch her and Riz because they were talking casually about weekend plans, ignoring me during the worst labor pains. It was almost as annoying as Riz enjoying my lunch because I was in too much pain to eat it.

What is family? If you ask a Japanese person, she will probably say something about blood connection; but for me, family is someone is you can trust, someone who is always there for you no matter what. Junko could not be more family to me if we shared the same blood. I could say the same of Ito Baba ("Baba" is like granny in English), my girls' Japanese grandma who drops everything when the girls are sick to watch them for us. She has had my kids over for sleepovers at her house, she goes to parent-teacher meetings when we can't, she makes dinner for us, and goes on family trips with us. Thanks to her, Riz and I are able to have pretty regular date nights. We introduce her as the kids' grandmother, and I really don't feel we have to explain because we love her as if she were a blood relative. My kids find as much comfort in her presence (sometimes more!) as they do ours. When we scold Emmy for bad behavior, she sometimes cries, "Ito Baba!!!!!!!!!!!!!!" Ito Baba is family.

Our girls with their beloved Mrs. Ito, affectionately called "Ito Baba."

There is Hirose-san, a wonderful neighbor I go walking with, one of many good friends I have made at the local bakery. She is always bringing over sweets for the kids, having parties for them and serving everyone around her. She fixed the broken doors on my house just because she wanted to. When I came home from a summer in the U.S, she had cut my grass, taken care of my yard, and collected my mail for me. This wealthy, privileged lady knows that real fulfillment, real contentment is not found in possessions but in relationships, in serving others.

There is Shiki-san, the *bento* (boxed lunch) maker at the local supermarket we befriended last year. She is always making stuff for my kids for their birthdays, Christmas, or just because. She has given them handmade quilts, handmade stuffed animals, bags, and picture frames. She gives us the head-ups when the *bentos* are going half-price, and she cooks our favorite foods for us.

She has no grandkids, so maybe my kids are like grandkids to her. I would never have met her if I weren't such a lousy cook.

Finally, there is Yoshiko, my Japanese soul sister. I met Yoshiko one day at the local bakery, too, when she came up to me and asked in perfect English where I was from. It turns out, she lived in the States when she was a kid, and like me, is caught between cultures. She knows what it is like to not really fit in anywhere, but to be able to be happy anyway. It took more than ten years for me to find a Japanese friend my age who I really connected with, who I could talk to about anything, and who shared my passion for exercise. We went rock climbing, I took her Pilates class, and we talk for hours about just about anything over our weekly lunches at a local curry place. I love her daughter and she loves mine, and we consider them to be family. Yoshiko is always telling me that I have helped her in so many ways, that I have changed her life. But she has helped me in so many ways, too, ways that I am not even sure I know about yet. I tell her all the time that everything happens for a reason, that there is no such thing as a coincidence. The day I met her, I had taken a day off to spend with Mia. Turns out, I forgot an important meeting at work that day. I got in a load of trouble for it, but I gained a wonderful friend.

Apple picking with Yoshiko and her family.

I have countless stories of other Japanese friends going above and beyond the call of duty to help us in our times of need. I wish I had space here to mention everyone who has ever done a kind thing for us. There are many reasons I love Japan, but I would not have stayed here nearly as long as I have if not for the people. The people are what make this a special place, and the people are the number one reason I don't want to leave yet.

But of course, Japanese people are not perfect. There are some aspects of the national personality that I do not understand, and I have been hurt several times by good friends. The one aspect that bothers me most is the unforgiving spirit I see in the hearts of many Japanese people. America has long ceased to be a Christian country, but the spirit of forgiveness, of making amends, of starting over still has a strong grip on many people there. But in Japan, I find that one often vows to never forgive a wrong, even if done unintentionally by someone considered a good friend. Most people in any culture would find it difficult to forgive someone who say, murdered their child, or even unintentionally caused his or her death. But the Japanese are particularly unforgiving of any offense caused to the *uchi*. Countless number of times I have read these words from a grieving father or mother in a Japanese newspaper; "I will never forgive him!" Once, I asked one of my best friends if she could find it in her heart to forgive me if I accidentally killed her mother in a car accident. She said no, that she could never forgive me. Her quick unequivocal response shocked me since she and I were so close, and that the hypothetical event was not intentional.

When I was talking to my Japanese friends about writing this chapter, two of them said the exact same thing. Yes, maybe the Japanese are bad at forgiveness, but not nearly as bad as the Chinese. They still hold a grudge against Japan for the atrocities committed during WWII. The Chinese would say that is because Japan has never really properly apologized. It just seems that grudges, hurt and pain can go on and on until someone decides to stop it. I once heard someone say that forgiveness is more for the wronged person than the person doing the wrong. Unforgiveness festers like a cancer that blackens your heart, while forgiving a person, who may not even want it, ask for it, or deserve it, frees the wounded person. I learned the Greek meaning of the word "grudge" contains the nuance of being entangled or entwined in something. Isn't that really what a grudge is? Your heart becomes so bitter and is so full of unforgiveness that you are entangled and most of all, not free. Forgiveness brings freedom for everybody involved. I wish I could help my Japanese friends who are being consumed by bitterness and anger to understand this truth, to be free from grudges and unforgiveness.

Japanese people also dislike conflict and confrontation, which can cause numerous problems in friendship. I have had several friendships in my life which have ended or been severely strained and I still have no idea why. I guess I did something to offend these friends, but rather than talk it out with me and give me a chance to apologize or change, they just cut me off and stop talking to me. What I think should have been a small bump in the road of friendship becomes a ten-car pile up with lots of casualties. I am not quite sure if I have done something unforgivable, or if it is just easier and more comfortable to avoid me and not have to deal with confrontation. I admit these experiences have left me a little wary of forming deep friendships with Japanese people. I wonder sometimes if all I have invested in a relationship might one day come crashing down and I will never know why. But, I love it here, and I love the people, so it is a risk I am willing to take.

I still think the Japanese are the most wonderful people I have ever met, and some of my most meaningful and fulfilling friendships are with Japanese people. While I have had my share of hurts, 99.9% of the people I have met here, and especially the people I have the honor to count as friends, would do anything for me at anytime. No matter where I live, I will encounter hurt, unnecessary grudges and unforgiveness. This is true of the United

States, Japan or anywhere else. But I can honestly say that there is no way my family would still be in Japan if not for the love and care that has been shown to us by the Japanese people. We have found our *uchi* here, and we are truly at home.

#5
Preschools

保育園

幼稚園

One cold winter day I found myself rushing around in a hurry. Unfortunately, this is not an uncommon occurrence since I have three young kids and I am a full-time working mommy. My daughters were once again taking forever to get ready, still shoeless despite me telling them 18 times or so to put their shoes on. I remember vividly one of them saying, "Mommy, can I wear socks?" I found myself snapping, "What are you talking about? You know you cannot wear socks to school!" The more I thought about it, the more ridiculous it sounded to me. Here I am, trying as hard as I can to keep my kids from catching the flu or one of the other million viruses circulating around Japanese schools in the winter, yet I am yelling at my kids for not wanting to be freezing and barefoot on cold hardwood floors in an old, unheated Japanese preschool. You see, socks are one of many articles of clothing banned at Japanese preschools. This may sound crazy and even cruel and maybe it is, but it is one of the only things I find ridiculous about the preschool system here. 95% of my experiences have been pure gold.

My oldest daughter Mia graduated from preschool last year. She entered when she was a year and a half old. I had taken six months off for maternity leave after she was born, and then Riz took a year off to be a stay-at-home dad. After we decided to put her into preschool, we began the process of researching the system in Japan. We found out that there are two types of care for preschool age children: *yochien* (kindergarten) and *hoikuen* (daycare or preschool). *Yochien* is for children from age three whose mothers are not working. Children generally attend only in the morning, but can stay later if arranged in advance with the school. *Hoikuen* is for children of working parents. They can attend Monday to Saturday from as early as 7 am to 6 pm. Of course, parents can bring their children earlier or later, but must take their kids by at least 9:30 in the morning and pick them up by 6 pm (We are pretty bad at getting our kids there on time, but the teachers give us a break!). In order for kids to attend *hoikuen*, both parents must produce proof from employers that they are working. Fees for *yochien* are set, and all students pay the same, but fees for *hoikuen* are based on the parents' joint income. Kids may start attending *hoikuen* from six months old, and up until the age of three kids are a little more expensive than kids older than three. Each city has different policies regarding fees and discounts for siblings, but in my city, we paid full cost for our first child, half-price for our second, and our third was free. The most we ever paid was a total of $800 a month for all three kids, but now we are only paying about $600 a month. We have friends with lower incomes who are paying less than $100 a month. This system is very fair, as the fees for public preschools are decided in similar ways to other social services.

By U.S. standards, $600 for full-time care for three children is probably considered quite a bargain, but it is even more so when you think about the level of care, attention, and education the kids get for that price. First, all public preschool teachers in Japan are required to be certified by the government, training for at least two years and then getting licensed. There is a security that parents can feel knowing that all teachers have been trained so rigorously. There are many privately run preschools in Japan, which do not have such strict standards for teachers. These schools are often much easier to get into than public preschools, but the cost is usually higher due to the convenience to parents. Public preschools are known to have long waiting lists, and sometimes children have to wait up to a year to be enrolled in areas with a lot of children. We visited five preschools around our home, and were told that we would have to wait more than a year to get our oldest into the one closest to our home. Even then, we were not guaranteed a space. With my husband going back to work, this was not an option, so we chose a preschool farther from our house (still only a five-minute drive), and are completely satisfied with it. It has not always been this way, though. It took us a while to get used to all the school policies, especially the one on fevers. In the beginning, it completely exasperated us.

You would think that fevers are like the plague as far as preschools are concerned. As soon as your kid's fever goes past 38.0 C (100.4 F), the school will call and ask you to come get her. I remember a period where I felt like I was getting a call everyday. I would leave work and go pick up the sick kid. As soon as we got home, the fever disappeared and my sick one played happily the rest of the day. Of course, if there is no way you can go pick up your child, the teachers will quarantine him in the principal's office until you can make it. Sometimes, they will call you just to tell you the child is feeling bad with a slight fever. You can buy some time asking them to keep an eye on it, and if her condition doesn't improve you will come after nap time.

My strategy as a working mom is this—no matter what, you have to make it past nap time! There is a huge difference between 11 am and 3 pm as far as getting work done. Besides, even if I go and pick up my sick child around lunchtime, the pediatrician is closed from 1 pm to 3 pm, so I figure it is better for my child to get rest at school anyway. I have to confess here to some less-than-ethical mommy behavior. Last spring, my husband had just left for the U.S. on a business trip, and I was trying to get some exercise in on the treadmill at lunchtime. I was feeling a little feverish, but I was planning on getting work done in the afternoon. A little after noon, I got a call on my cell. I wasn't aware it was ringing, so when I looked at my phone later, I saw the missed call. It was from the preschool. I started plotting. The kids were finishing up lunch and getting ready for nap time. I couldn't take her (wasn't sure yet which kid was sick, but knew it had to be one of them) to the doctor until three. So I confess that I waited until after I knew she had fallen asleep, which was about 12:30, before returning the call. Sure enough, Emmy had just fallen asleep. I told them I would get her at three, and take her to the doctor. Turned out, she had the chicken pox, and I had the flu. She had a good nap, and I got a lot of work done before three. Bad mommy? Maybe, but many of my friends have confessed to similar behavior.

As annoying as the constant calls are, I am very thankful that the schools try to keep sick kids home. Other kindergartens are even stricter. If one child has the flu, all the siblings must stay home. Some sicknesses are inevitable since there are a lot of little kids with germs playing together all day long in a closed environment. My oldest Mia was sick all the time, but now she rarely gets sick, because she caught pretty much every disease known to humankind when she was younger. Of course, if the kids are catching everything, the parents get it too. I had had the stomach flu maybe twice in my life before kids; now I get it almost every year. Going to preschool builds up the immune system for kids, but unfortunately not for parents. While I realize some sicknesses are inevitable, I still appreciate the preschool trying to contain outbreaks as much as possible. I remember visiting one private preschool and kids with runny noses were all over the place in a little room. The principal told me with pride that a child with a fever was welcome. That visit didn't last long.

Private school teachers are also not required to have such rigorous training. Five years ago, a private kindergarten in my city took some students on an outing. Through a teacher's carelessness, a two-year old child was left inside a scorching hot bus in the middle of August. When they returned to look for him, they found him unconscious and not breathing, but the teacher moved the bus into the shade and changed his diaper before calling 911. The child died. I know first-hand that sometimes people do crazy things when they panic, but this kind of reaction is hard for me to grasp.

When I talked to the teachers at my daughter's school about this, they said it would never happen at a public preschool because the teachers are trained and trained to constantly count the children to make sure they are all present. They said they would not have left that bus if a child was missing. Hearing stories like this make me glad I chose to enroll my kids in a public preschool. I know that sometimes accidents are inevitable, and that something bad could happen to my children at any school. I mean, if you think about it, you are entrusting your precious children to relative strangers, who as much as they care about your kids, don't have near the affection for them as you do. However, I feel as good as I can, and I am at peace that I have put my kids in the safest environment possible.

As far as what they do all day, it is much more of an educational environment than I expected. From a young age, they read the kids stories, do crafts, puzzles, dexterity activities, and flash cards. They teach them Japanese folk talks, nursery rhymes and children's songs. They toilet train them, too, taking them to the potty from as young as six months old. Of course, they don't always pee in the potty, but they are trying to instill the habit in them. They look pretty cute, too, on those little potties. Mia learned to read and write in Japanese at preschool. In fact, her Japanese is so good that I am much more worried about her English than her Japanese. When they get older, they also regularly attend origami class at a local community center. They have exercise class. Their days are full of activities.

They spend a lot of time outside, too. They plant vegetables, cultivate them, and harvest them. Then, the kids in the older classes make lunch for everyone using the veggies they grew. They play in the pool everyday in the summer. They are outside running around whenever possible, and they NEVER watch TV. They even roast sweet potatoes that the kids planted themselves in the school yard during the fall. My kids, like most Japanese kids, are crazy about sweet potatoes; Abby is legendary at the preschool for the number of sweet potatoes she can consume.

Lunch and an afternoon snack are included in the preschool fees. The mainly Japanese meals are balanced and healthy. Thanks to eating at school everyday, my kids love most Japanese foods, especially fish. I wish I could say the same thing about myself! They love Japanese food so much that it is always hard when we visit the States. They don't even like stuff Japanese kids like: pizza, spaghetti, hotdogs, sandwiches, bagels. They would choose rice and fish over hot dogs and fries any day, especially Mia. I remember laughing once during a visit to the States as I watched my kids eat plain white rice for breakfast while their cousins were downing peanut butter bagels.

A teacher prepares roasted sweet potatoes.

The preschools teach kids from a young age to eat and drink by themselves, first with forks, spoons, and bottles, but gradually progressing to chopsticks and cups. They learn table manners. They learn to clean up after themselves. It is amazing.

The thing I love the most as a parent is the wide variety of crafts that they do. Every March, the kids come home with a huge bag of crafts that they have done throughout the year, including Christmas, Halloween, and New Years, as well as a variety of Japanese holidays and festivals. Many times, they preserve their handprints or footprints in paint--priceless memories for mommy and daddy. My oldest daughter was even taught how to knit a scarf during her final year! That one was icing on the cake for me. I mean, I can't even do that.

And then, there are the school outings. A couple times a year, the oldest class takes trips to nearby parks, museums or theaters. They even go on an overnight outing, in which they go hiking, grass skiing, and hear ghost stories. Other events where parents attend include the yearly sports day, winter recital, and parent/child picnic. Watching my kids develop, interact with their classmates, and speak Japanese so much better than I do is a constant source of pride for me. These bonding times with the kids, and the chance to interact with other parents are some of the most enjoyable times of the year. Except, of course, when I have to make the dreaded *bento*.

The *bento* strikes fear in the heart of all new mothers, especially this American one. Translated loosely as "boxed lunch," the *bento* is nothing like the lunches packed by American mothers for their children. When I was little, my lunch would typically have a sandwich, apple, maybe some chips or raw carrots and a juice box. I am not sure, but I am guessing that it took my mom about five minutes to prepare it. That kind of lunch would horrify the Japanese mother. One of the major responsibilities for Japanese mothers and wives is to prepare healthy, balanced, delicious, and very importantly, aesthetically pleasing lunches for her husband and children. While most convenience stores sell *bentos*, it is not acceptable for most moms to buy them. It is too expensive and well, kind of a cultural taboo. Mothers cook. They do laundry. They take care of their kids. And they make *bentos*.

Recently, the increase in working mothers is probably changing this, but most mothers I know still prepare *bentos* at home. I remember the first time I had to take a *bento*. I bought one at a convenience store, and then transferred it to a *bento* box so that no one would bust me. I have a sneaking suspicion that I am not the only mommy in Japan that has done this.

The standard *bento* will contain rice, fish or other meat, some kind of veggie, a pickle, and maybe egg. The intimidating thing is how stinking beautiful Japanese mothers make these things. I have no idea how they taste, but they sure do look good.

Recently, character *bentos* have become popular in Japan. Moms will make *bentos* with a character theme; for example, a baseball theme or Mickey Mouse. They can make a *bento* look like a baseball field, or a farm or anything else they want. It is amazing.

My daughters and I made this at a bento-making class.

Once, I took my girls to a character *bento* class. We learned how to make a pig-themed *bento* box. The rice ball was the head; ham cut diagonally and rolled up was the ears; small wieners slices were the eyes, with the eyeballs formed by making a hole in the wiener with a straw. It was really cute, really fun, and really exhausting. I mean, come on! Japanese moms do this kind of thing every single day! I only have to do it a couple times a year (for now). The woman who taught the class told me that she makes *bentos* like these everyday for her kids, and she really enjoys it. I guess that is my problem. I have never really enjoyed cooking, and I do it only because I love my family and want them to eat well. I never cooked as a child because I was always out of the house at some sports practice. I couldn't even make spaghetti, a grilled cheese or a hamburger when I got married. My husband is a saint. In fourteen years of marriage, he has never once complained about my cooking. Not once. I am better at cooking now, but I still don't really enjoy it.

This dislike of cooking has transferred to the making of the *bento*. I have gotten pretty good at making cute *bentos*, but I still get stressed out by it. The first time I had to make a *bento* I was so stressed that one of my supermom friends offered to do it for me. After thinking about it (for about two seconds) I accepted. She made gorgeous *bentos* for all of us, complete with dessert, wet wipes, and chopsticks, all loaded neatly into a picnic basket. The second time I had to do it, I broke out in a sweat, then accompanied my veteran mommy friend Junko to the supermarket for a *bento*-making lesson. Much to my surprise, we spent most of our time in the frozen food section. She said it is the easy way to go, the kids like it, and no one will ever find you out. She swore that Japanese moms do the same thing, even though they may not admit it. I relaxed, and made a pretty cute *bento* if I do say so myself. I felt even better when I saw another family bring McDonald's to the picnic. Yes, *bentos* are a scary creature, but thanks to the wonderful preschool lunches, I only have to do it a couple times a year.

My 5-year old, Abby, with her favorite teacher.

Anyway, back to singing the praises of preschools. While the education and nutritious meals are great, the thing that is by far the best aspect of the schools is the staff. The teachers are awesome, and they really love my children. There is nothing too small to talk to me about when it concerns my kid. I don't know how many times the teachers have apologized to me at the end of the day because my child fell down or got hit by another kid, or had some other mishap. Most of the time, I couldn't even tell when looking at the injured body part, and my child was not complaining. They pay close attention to the health, growth and development of the children, and know them all so well. They genuinely love each and every child. I know with certainty that every teacher there cares about my children and is committed to taking care of them. Not only are they concerned with their physical growth, but they also train them in social skills to treat each other with respect and compassion. They love the kids, but are not shy to rebuke bad behavior. They are so detailed and precise in everything, a trait that probably leads to one of the only annoying things about the preschool system.

I have pretty much gotten used to dealing with the ridiculously detailed requests, but I was at my wit's end at the beginning. It seemed, first of all, that every article of clothing my child owned was not appropriate for preschool: hooded shirts or jackets were dangerous because the other kids might yank them. I thought this was crazy until I read a story in the newspaper where a young child was strangled when the string from his hood got caught on a piece of playground equipment. After that, I figured the teachers knew what they were talking about. *Onesies* are bad because kids cannot potty themselves (I rebelled against this one until my kids were about two! I mean, a one-year old doesn't need to potty and then reattach his Onesie!). Skirts are bad for the same reason—potty interference and playground interference. Jeans are too tight and hard for kids to move around in. Sandals are dangerous. If pants are too long, hem them or sew them. Rolling up is bad. Also too dangerous. The most ridiculous one was the ban on socks because, you guessed it! Socks are dangerous. The kids may slip and fall down on the hardwood floors. So, kids go barefoot in the winter because, as you know, Japanese people do not wear shoes inside.

Japanese kids in general don't wear many layers in winter. I always think kids look like they are freezing here. They will wear shorts in winter.   Conversely, Japanese adults, especially men, almost never wear shorts. No matter how hot it is, they don't wear shorts because shorts are considered childish. Japanese attire is determined by the calendar, not the weather.   As an American, I will wear shorts in November if it is warm. I am met with the inevitable, "Aren't you cold?" I get this even if it is in the mid-80s. Conversely, girls can get away with wearing shorts and knee boots in winter because it is "fashion," but if you wear a short-sleeved shirt, you are viewed either as a cultural rebel or a crazy person. Last year, I did an experiment at work. I decided to wear shorts, t-shirts and sandals into the fall until I couldn't stand it anymore. October was warm, but my students were already breaking out turtlenecks, sweaters and boots. But, because it was relatively warm, I just got, "*Sensei*, aren't you cold?" November got a little chillier, so I got much more frequent, "*Sensei*! It's cold!" They were wearing down jackets and scarves at this point. Finally, at the end of November, I broke down and wore socks for the first time that fall. But this experiment helped me to see that even how people dressed was determined by cultural expectations, not by the weather.

In addition to the regulations about clothing at the preschool, offhanded comments about my parenting style sometimes got under my skin. For example, once I went to pick up Mia for something, I cannot even remember what. My younger daughters were sleeping, and needed to sleep, or they would be grumpy later. In fact, they didn't even know I was there. A teacher made a comment like, "You should come as quickly as you can to get Abby and Emmy because they will be sad you didn't get them, too." I felt like shooting back, "Not unless you tell them I came for their sister and left them behind!" I realize now, that the teachers meant no harm. Our cultures are just different, and we do things in different ways. I feel that it is important to do things sometimes with each child individually, preserving that one-on-one time. The

Japanese probably see this as unfair to the child left behind. Of course, I spend time with Abby and Emmy alone, too, at other times, but the teachers probably just saw it as me giving one child preferential treatment over the other.

There are other things they do that are mildly annoying: telling me to cut my child's bangs; telling me her fingernails need to be cut shorter. My American friend jealously guards her authority to make decisions like this for her daughter, which led to a clash with her daughter's elementary school teacher when she decided to get her daughter's ears pierced. Talk about rebellious behavior! Japanese schoolchildren, until graduation from high school, are not allowed to get their ears pierced. This was a very important issue for my friend, and she would not back down. My two oldest, Mia and Abby, got their ears pierced last summer and enjoyed it the six weeks we were in the U.S. But of course, the moment they returned to school we were told to take out the earrings. I responded at the preschool that we couldn't because the holes would close. So we compromised and the teachers put Band Aids over Abby's ears, supposedly because it was dangerous if the earrings fell out and the little babies swallowed them. I could kind of see the point. No, not really, actually. What are the odds of that? There is a much greater chance a baby not restrained in a car seat will be hurt in a car accident, but I will vent about that in the next chapter.

For two days we put Band Aids over Abby's earrings, but on the second day, when we tried to take the Band Aids off, they caused her ears to bleed. Abby was so traumatized she hated her earrings and wanted to take them out. The elementary school did not even give us that option. Take them out, they said. We decided it was too much of a hassle, and I had to save my energy for when the school tried to make me serve on the PTA. You have to pick your battles here.

The way I see it, Japanese preschools, and probably all schools for that matter, are much more involved and opinionated about issues that would be seen as personal decisions in the U.S. But at the same time, this involvement in my children's lives is also why they know and love them so much. So, like many things in Japan, sometimes the things that annoy me most about preschool, are also the things I love the best. In case you are wondering what happened to my rebellious friend and her daughter with pierced ears, the school eventually backed down but they were not happy about it.

All told, the wonderful things I have experienced in the Japanese preschool system far outweigh the small annoyances. The quality of care, education and nutrition are top notch, and the love the teachers have for the children is unquestioned. The time, too, that they spend making memories is unbelievable. Last year, Mia graduated from preschool. In addition to spending countless hours decorating the classroom for the occasion, the teachers made a high quality, personalized scrapbook for each child with memories of his or her last year in preschool. It had to have taken hours to put together. There was also a graduation book in which all the teachers wrote messages to the kids, and drawings and messages from each child were also included. I was so moved by the time, thought and planning that went into preparing these gifts. The minor irritation I feel sometimes is more than worth it when I think about the wonderful experiences and growth that Mia had during the last four years. The Japanese preschool system is the best, and I will shout from the rooftops about how wonderful it is to anyone who will listen.

Part II.

Five Things I Don't Get

理解ができない五つのこと

#1

Car Seat
Anyone?

チャイルドシート
を使わないこと

When I was pregnant with each of my three girls, I tried to maintain a pretty active lifestyle, both for myself and for the baby. This included regular stuff like continuing to work and go about daily chores, as well as doing maternity aerobics and walking almost everyday. The exercise part horrified some of my Japanese friends. "You are crazy," one of my midwife friends said of maternity aerobics. "I cannot even do this, and I am not pregnant!" People were amazed to see me walking every morning, reaching for high stuff (there is an old wives' tale in Japan that this can cause the umbilical cord to get wrapped around the baby's neck, causing stillbirth), and walking around with no maternity supporter around my waist. This *hara obi,* literally "stomach band," is considered one of the most essential components of maternity attire. It not only supports the growing tummy, but also keeps it warm.

The Japanese think letting your tummy get cold causes every sickness known to man. Most Japanese women, on *Inu no hi* (Day of the Dog—don't ask me, I have no idea!) sometime around the midpoint of pregnancy, start wrapping their tummies in the *hara obi* and keep it there until childbirth. Recently, many moms have been forgoing this tradition, but most people still believe that this wrapping provides extra support and protection for the baby. However, it is not just moms, but also kids who are warned against cold tummies. There is this pediatrician in town famous for rebuking mothers when they bring in sick kids, blaming them for letting their kids get cold tummies. Before coming to Japan, I had never in my life heard of cold tummies blamed for illness. Have you?

Anyway, I was very active up until childbirth with all three kids. My youngest was induced due to IUGR, but I was still relatively healthy throughout the pregnancy with her. During my first pregnancy, I remember telling some friends I was going to attend the school festival nearby the weekend before my due date.

I was on maternity leave, which in for me started four weeks before the due date and continued eight weeks after.

Believe or not, taking maternity leave in Japan is mandatory for full-time employees, whether it is paid leave or not. When I was pregnant with my second child, I was just going to use my paid vacation days for a month or so because my employer did not provide paid maternity leave. Imagine my shock when I was told that it was a law that I take maternity leave, UNPAID maternity leave!! Granted, I would be reimbursed 60% from my health care plan later, but I did not receive any income for the actual time I was not working. In addition, even though I wasn't getting paid, I still had to pay my monthly healthcare premium. I am sure that this law was enacted to protect women from abusive employers, put in place to guarantee the new mother would have a job to go back to after giving birth.

Many employers probably ignore this law, but it was clear my employer wouldn't. There are still very few wives in Japan who are the breadwinners for their families like I am for mine, so I doubt the Japanese government considered the considerable financial hardship they were imposing on families like mine when they passed this law. My husband was teaching part-time at a university, but since Abby was born during summer vacation, he wasn't making any money either. So while it was wonderful being at home with Riz and the new baby for almost two months, we had to pay for basic necessities like rent and utilities from our savings.

So, I am on maternity leave, pretty bored because I am not working, the house is spotless and all the preparations for the new baby were ready. Going to the school festival every year is one of the highlights of my year. The students work so hard and do everything, from the planning to the organizing to running all the events and food stalls. I like to go every year and support them and all their hard work. My friends were SHOCKED that I would be venturing out eight days before my due date, walking a horrendously far eight minutes from my house to the school grounds. What if you go into labor at the festival? What will you do? Is it safe? I assured them that I would be fine, considering the distance from the school to my hospital was the same as my house to the hospital. I assured them there would be no danger to the baby or to me. Much to my friends' relief, I didn't go into labor that weekend, but I did have Mia five days later. I am sure that it made my friends happy that I was home in bed when contractions came, and I made it to the hospital with plenty of time to spare.

The point I want to make here is this: Japanese women are extremely careful during pregnancy. They do not do anything that they think may harm the baby. The aversion to exercise has been changing recently, as I have seen clinics organize maternity exercise classes, and sports clubs offer maternity swimming classes. Doctors are also encouraging pregnant women to be more active, both to keep weight gain in check and to contribute to overall mental and physical health. However, the prevailing attitude is still that pregnancy is almost like a sickness, not a state or condition, and women who have this sickness should take it easy. Most of my friends avoid carrying anything heavy, exercise, and in some cases, driving. I find that the culture promotes the pampering of pregnant women, and often, women's mothers will come to take care of everything during the early stages of pregnancy when morning sickness is the worst. Many women will even quit working during pregnancy to ensure that the pregnancy has the absolute best chance of success. As an American, I can just imagine asking my mom to take care of me for weeks during morning sickness. Suck it up. I can just imagine her saying that.

This caution extends into labor and childbirth, where most women want to avoid any kind of medical intervention if possible. I think one reason is that they feel the need to experience the pain and horrible suffering they think is necessary to say "I AM NOW A MOTHER!! HEAR ME ROAR" (The roaring usually happens since they don't use pain medication!). Using epidurals or having a C-section will lessen this accomplishment in their eyes. However, another reason is that they do not want to do anything that will possibly harm the baby. Even though research has shown that epidurals pose very little risk to the baby, and in many cases, C-sections are recommended for babies in distress, there is still reluctance among Japanese mothers for any kind of medical intervention.

I delivered all three of my girls with no epidurals. I wish I could say it was because of my superhuman ability to *gaman* (endure or persevere) through the pain like Japanese mommies, but in all honesty, I asked for an epidural all three times, but all three girls were born before it could be administered. By the time the third one was born and I was screaming epidural, the midwives just stood there laughing at me. There was one lady in the hospital with me who was in labor for almost two days. She was so traumatized by the pain of childbirth that she was unsure if she wanted any more children. I suggested an epidural next time, told her she wouldn't feel nearly as much pain, and could still experience the joy of having a baby. She looked at me like she had never in a million years thought of that one. I heard that in the big cities like Tokyo, epidural use is increasing. Those sophisticated Tokyoites have been enlightened and realized, "Hey!! I can go through this whole thing totally pain free, and still have a cute little baby to show for it. Sign me up!" Of course, this being a rebellious thing to do, it is not covered by national health care. Patients are expected to cough up about 500 bucks for an epidural, which due to the Japanese aversion to anesthesia in general, is usually just a pain reducer, not a pain remover like it is in the U.S. In my country home in Kyushu, only about 5% of women at my clinic choose to have an epidural.

So, Japanese mothers are fierce about protecting their babies, right? Sure sounds that way. So imagine my horror at seeing new parents drive their precious little bundle of joy home with no car seat, either holding the baby or even worse, placing him or her in a little, cushioned Moses basket on the floor. It seems that the possibility that a car accident could snatch away this euphoria of having a new baby is not even on the radar. A few years back, Britney Spears horrified the U.S. public when she drove around with her toddler in her lap, but I see this kind of thing all the time here and nobody even blinks.

In Japan, most women will go stay with their mothers for the first month after being released from the hospital. Their mothers will do everything—cook, clean, laundry. The new mother is expected to only take care of the baby and herself. One of my friend's mothers is so strict that she is not even allowed to read or use a computer during this period because it is too much of a strain on her frail body. So, because of this, most people will rationalize not installing a car seat right away, since, with the exception of going from the hospital to mother's home, the baby will not be in a car until he is at least one month old. Others say that a baby is too small and wiggly to put in a car seat.

I once saw a new Japanese mother driving while holding a newborn baby in the crook of her arm. I am not sure how old this baby was, but he definitely did not have head control. I am thinking he was about three weeks old. I thought I had seen it all here, but even that shocked me. Even my three-year old daughter said, "Mommy, that is really bad, isn't it!" She said it really loudly, and at the time I was glad she said it in English so no one could understand her, but later I thought, "Maybe it would have been better if she had said it in Japanese so this mother would have to think about her crazy behavior."

Once new parents finally get around to installing car seats, many times they do one of two things, both of which could get an American in loads of trouble. First, they will put in a car seat in the rear passenger seat, but it will be front-facing, not rear-facing. American standards recommend that a child stay in the rear-facing position until 10 kg or one year old. Recently, experts are recommending that regardless of age, a child should be at least 10 kg before turning around a car seat. Japanese mothers who place babies in front-facing seats say that the baby will panic or cry if he or she cannot see mommy. That is another reason they do Unbelievable Thing #2. Many parents will put a car seat into the front passenger seat. This way, the baby will be relaxed if he can see mommy and will not cry as much. If he does cry, mommy, being nearby can comfort baby quickly and easily. Being a trained linguist fascinated by language usage, I decided to look at the warnings on the visor above the passenger seats in Japanese and U.S. cars. I found a fascinating contrast. In Japanese cars sold in the U.S., the warning says, "NEVER place a car seat or a child under 8 years old in the passenger seat, as the child may be suffocated by the airbag." The warning in the car sold in Japan says (my translation): "As much as possible, you should avoid placing a car seat in the passenger seat. The rear seat is the safest place for children." AS MUCH AS POSSIBLE??? This is the land of situational ethics for crying out loud. I can hear the excuses now. "My baby is crying, so it is not possible." Or "I have to put the groceries in the back, so it is not possible." The government bears the brunt of the responsibility for this in my mind due to their lack of regulation. With all the other laws to protect children, the least they could do is get car manufacturers to take out the AS MUCH AS POSSIBLE.

Car visor with instructions about car seat usage.

I am often amazed at the harsh language Japanese use in certain situations and soft language used in others. For example, the laws against drunk driving are incredibly harsh with severe penalties. Recently, a new law requiring passengers in the rear seats to wear seat belts was enacted. Yet, I have never heard of anyone getting a ticket for not having children properly restrained. When I went to the mandatory two-hour lecture to renew my drivers' license, I was horrified that most of the time was spent giving strategies on how to get a gold license, which was obtainable after five years of no traffic violations. The other time was used to address drunk driving, which is severely punished in Japan, and carelessness. There was never any mention of using car seats for children.

To be fair, many parents do buy very high tech, safe car seats for their children and use them properly. However, I can say with pretty high certainty, that very few parents use car seats properly once their children are toddlers. When I pick my girls up from preschool, most of their friends, from ages two to six, are unrestrained, many times not even using seat belts. All the time, I see six-year old kids holding two-year old brothers or sisters in the front seat; I see little kids climbing all over the dashboard while their parents are driving; I see Grandma holding an infant in the rear seat. I am amazed that a country so careful about protecting pregnant women, and so zealous about the health and education of their children, can be so reckless when it comes to automobile safety and children.

My girls, ages 7, 5, and 3 still ride in car seats. My two oldest are now in booster seats, while my youngest is using a toddler car seat. To be entirely honest and candid, there have been times when I have been reckless too, whether due to being frazzled, inconvenienced, or just plain lazy. Or perhaps, maybe I too have been influenced by the lax car seat usage in Japan. I remember one time when my infant daughter was screaming her head off while my husband maneuvered the busy streets of

Fukuoka. Frazzled to the core, I took her out of her car seat and nursed her, an incredibly reckless thing to do, and I am thankful there were no dire consequences. At other times, my kids have ridden with friends who have no car seats for them. Sometimes, when going to the supermarket close to our house, I will let one of my two older girls ride in the front passenger seat with me.

As I have at times done some of the same irresponsible things I am condemning here, I am in no place to judge. The difference, though, is that I think most Japanese parents are totally unaware of the danger they are putting their children in. I, on the other hand, am aware, but irresponsible. I think this makes me even more accountable because I know the dangers and sometimes still do it anyway. I can honestly say that my children are properly restrained 95% of the time, but who knows that an accident will not happen in that 5% of the time they are not?

Japanese children are very rarely properly restrained. This scares me and flabbergasts me at the same time. I love this country, so I take advantage of every opportunity to educate and encourage my friends to restrain their kids better. Not surprisingly, very rarely are they even aware that it is dangerous to place a car seat in the front. I think the ultimate responsibility is with the government, to not only make the laws but to enforce them. I am told that there are laws about the use of car seats, but I have never once seen them enforced. In any country, a law that in not enforced will not be followed. Japan is not any different. Japanese people routinely park in handicapped parking spaces; Americans don't. Is this because Americans are more moral than the Japanese? I don' t think so. In America, you will get a five hundred dollar fine within an hour of parking in one of those spots because it is a strictly enforced law and everybody knows it. In Japan, it isn't enforced and everybody knows it. The bottom line is, people fear punishment, so the Japanese government should punish improper child restraint like they punish failure to use seat belts or drunk driving. The government also needs to educate

114

people better on car seat safety, perhaps using the time spent in mandatory drivers' license renewal classes more wisely. Japanese people cherish their children, and they would never put them in such danger if they were made to think more deeply about how reckless their improper car seat usage is. My heart's desire for them is that they would protect these precious children after they are born as much as they do while they are still in their mommy's tummy.

#2
No Central Heating

霜焼けができる
ぐらい家が寒い

I really, really hate being cold. Let me say that again. I hate being cold. I hate winter with a passion and wish that one day God would call me to be a missionary to Hawaii, Guam or even Okinawa. One of my most vivid memories growing up in the frigid mountains of Southwest Virginia was fighting with my younger brother over who got to sit in front of the kerosene heater. My parents were not poor--they were both teachers (okay, maybe close to poor!)--but they were very frugal. As a young kid, I thought they were cheapskates to be honest. I wanted to eat out more, take more vacations, get more Christmas presents like all my friends. My mom used to always say, "They may get more presents, but they are going to be paying back college loans for ten years, and you won't." Of course, this held no meaning to a ten-year old. Yeah, whatever, Mom. Gimme the toys.

Of course, as an adult, I view my Mom as a wise, old sage and most of the things she said that annoyed me as a child seem like pearls of wisdom now. Of course, she was right about the college loans, just like she was right about everything else 99.9% of the time. My teacher parents put three kids through college without borrowing a dime. Of course, in order to do that, they had to be really frugal. I was crazy about cantaloupe in high school, and I wanted to eat it every day for breakfast during summer. Mom was happy to feed my melon addiction, as long they cost less than $1.50, preferably 99 cents.

After coming to Japan, I was shocked by the prices of fruit. Many fruits like watermelon, cantaloupe, honeydew, and grapes are more often given as gifts than eaten at home. I remember taking a picture of a $100 cantaloupe at a market and sending it to my Mom. In 2008, the two first Yubari cantaloupes of the season sold at an auction for $26,000. Even spend-thrifty me thinks that is crazy. My parents are awesome and I love them to death. I respect them more than they will ever know, and they have molded me into the person I am today. By far the hardest part of being in Japan is being away from them and my two brothers. I just wanted to make sure I didn't finish this book without giving a shout out to the folks. That just wouldn't be right. I wonder how much of the money Mom saved on all those cantaloupes over the years went towards getting me through college debt free...

But as a kid, although I loved my parents very much, I had yet to come to appreciate just how awesome they were, and how much my future self would benefit from their frugality. One of the ways my parents' frugality played out was in their reluctance to use our central heating system. They kept the temperature set very low and we just used a little kerosene heater and a lot of blankets. To this day, I have a negative image of kerosene. I remember my Dad's hands always smelling of kerosene, and sometimes the kerosene would spill in the car. He would start yelling about how much he hated kerosene, and the car would reek of it for days. Obviously, he didn't hate it enough to crank up the central heating, though.

I remember as a kid going out and shoveling snow to earn some extra cash with my brother, coming home frozen to the core. We would thaw out in front of that little kerosene heater, often getting heat rash on our legs because we got too close. I didn't know anyone else who used kerosene, although other families in my freezing town must have. Because it seemed to me such an archaic way to heat a house, I thought I had left kerosene behind me forever when I came to Japan. Imagine my shock and disdain coming to Japan and seeing people everywhere smelling up their houses with that reeking substance. That was in the living room, the only room with a temperature above freezing. The rest of the rooms in the house were cold enough to both see your breath and refrigerate your food. "What the heck?!?", I thought. I thought I was in the most technologically advanced country in the world, not in Siberia!

I came to Japan for the first time in the fall of 1997. Staying with my host family for six months, I had my first experience sleeping on a *futon* and sleeping under the enormous futon comforter the Japanese call *kakebuton*. This was my first winter away from central heating, and somehow under that mammoth comforter, I was able to sleep relatively well. Six months later, I got married, and joined my husband in his $80 a month subsidized apartment.

Needless to say, there were several uncomfortable reasons it was only $80 a month. To start with it was very small. It only had two rooms and a kitchen, what the Japanese call a 2K apartment. However, since there were only two of us, that was not a problem. The problem was the heat, or rather, the lack of it. You see, Japanese houses, with the exception of those on the northern island of Hokkaido, are not equipped with central heating. It is not because the Japanese cannot afford it; on the contrary, Japan is one of the richest, most technologically advanced nations in the world. They simply see central heating as wasteful. Why would you spend money and natural resources heating rooms that you are not using? Most of the time, they will keep the heater on in the living room when they are at home. Of course, it is dangerous to keep it on when you are out, so most people come home from work to a freezing house. An hour or so before bedtime, they will turn on the heaters set to a timer in the bedroom to make it bearable enough to sleep. Then, after they have drifted off to la la land, the heater will automatically turn off because it is also dangerous to sleep with it on. And again, they wake up to a freezing house.

So, thanks to this Spartan, utilitarian way of thinking, I found myself newly married, in love, and absolutely freezing. It was so cold in our apartment that I could see my breath. I regularly went to sleep wearing ski pants, a fleece sweatshirt and a bathrobe. Our living room window was broken, so it was fairly windy in there. I would say drafty, but no, it was windy. Once, it snowed and the snow drifted in through a kitchen vent and formed a nice pile on our kitchen floor. We spent three miserably cold winters in Kobe, with only a little electric heater and love for each other to keep us warm. We had to turn this off (the heater, not the love!) to be safe, so getting out of bed in the morning was torture, especially since we did not have a shower to warm us up. Nope, no shower in our $80 a month apartment. If you remember from chapter one, our first little love nest had only a bathtub with a complex mechanism for heating cold water that didn't work if our timing was off by even a millisecond. Freezing my buns off even though I was wearing ski pants and bathrobe, I had little patience for that tub on cold winter mornings. More often than not, I gave up after a couple tries.

In 2003, we returned to Japan, with better jobs and a better living situation. At first, we lived in public housing and were warmed with our first electric wall heater. Heaven! We also had a *kotatsu* heated table, a cool Japanese invention with a heater underneath, that, when covered with a blanket, traps the heat and keeps your legs warm and toasty. They are great, but take up a ton of space, so we got rid of it after our kids were born. They have lost popularity a bit in modern Japan, maybe because they take up so much space, or maybe because they keep many people, from housewives to students, from getting any work done. They are so toasty that people crawl under the *kotatsu* blanket and fall asleep while eating oranges (not really sure why oranges are the *kotatsu* food of choice). Anyway, with all our new heating contraptions, and the fact that Kyushu was farther south than Kobe, the Japanese winters were much more bearable for us this time around. In addition, my school was new, so each room, including my office, could be set to a toasty 78 degrees Fahrenheit. After our first daughter was born, we moved to our first house, thrilled to have arrived at last. A house! What a blessing.

Or curse, if you think about trying to heat an old, two-story wooden house with a huge living room. As much as we tried to avoid it, we realized that kerosene was our only option. Japanese houses, especially older wooden ones like ours, are insulated poorly and freezing cold in the winter. Especially in Kyushu, homes are built to stay cool during the hot summers. Well, in that case, they will naturally be freezing cold in the winter. Our house was cold, really cold. It reminded me of our days in Kobe. I didn't want to leave the living room because the rest of the house was as cold as it was outside, maybe colder. Our bedroom was miserably cold. The bathroom was cold. The kitchen was cold. The only place that wasn't cold was the *ofuro,* the most important place in the house. I would stay in there forever to stay warm. Getting out was horrible. Cold again. Oh yeah, the toilet wasn't cold either. My husband's splurge with that year's winter bonus was a heated toilet seat. That is one invention my tush is very dependent on. A couple years ago when we went to the States for Christmas, my bottom cried out in shock every time the call of nature came.

But in general, we were cold. The living room, however, was warm. Kerosene heaters are stinky, messy, and bad for your health, but they do a surprisingly good job at warming up a room fast. Kerosene is also much more economical than the other two options, electric heaters and gas heaters. So, as much as I hated kerosene, we decided to try it for a year and see how it went.

After our second daughter, Abby, was born, I decided these fumes just had to be bad for our kids. So, I sold our kerosene heaters, bought another electric heater, and declared that the Crescinis were going kerosene-free. Hallelujah! Finally. Unfortunately, there were two small problems: electric heaters are expensive, and they don't really do a good job at heating large rooms. So, while our electricity bill doubled, our comfort level was halved. We were paying more but were colder than ever. Our electric bill was so much higher than our neighbors' that a guy from the power company came by to make sure we were aware of our crazy overuse, and to rule out any miscalculation. I assured him that there was no miscalculation, we were very aware, and also very willing to spend the extra money to stay warm. Shocked as he was by our enthusiasm to waste both energy as money, he uttered a polite thank you and was on his way. We managed to endure that winter, but the following winter, we swallowed our pride and went back to kerosene, regretting our overzealous idealism, which caused us to sell our nice kerosene heaters at a way-too-cheap price. We decided to supplement our energy-sucking electric heaters with kerosene heaters.

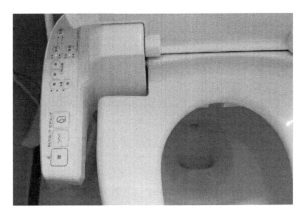

My heated toilet seat: the warmest seat in the house.

So anyway, my question is, why is it so dang cold everywhere? Houses are cold. Schools are cold. Supermarkets, trains, post offices, gyms. Cold. Cold. Cold. I went to an orientation at my daughter's elementary school last February, which was held in the school gym. By the time it finished two hours later, I was a popsicle, frozen to the core. There was one lone industrial-looking kerosene heater for the entire gym, like that made much of a difference. I felt like I was in the Russian countryside. I was told that the classrooms are not even heated until it gets below 10 degrees C (50 F). How can students study in an environment like that? My kids' daycare is also freezing, as my barefoot kids can tell you. I tried to shoot hoops at the university gym once during winter, but I couldn't move my fingers so I gave up. Even supermarket checkers wear football jackets to work. Now remember, Kyushu is not any colder than my hometown in Virginia; on the contrary, Virginia is much colder. The difference is that in Kyushu, I cannot escape the cold. It is cold in my house, my work, the supermarket, the train, and the bus. It is cold everywhere. The only time I am not cold is when I sit on my toilet seat or take a bath.

There is nothing worse than the five beeps on my kerosene heater, followed by a countdown, starting at ten minutes. Ten minutes of kerosene left. Then it will be out, and I (or if I can suffer until he wakes up, my husband) will trek out into the frigid morning to refill the heater, hoping not to spill on my clothes or hands and stink up my house for the next few hours. Of course, sometimes I have to wait because it is too dark to see and I can't fill it up until the sun comes up. I often marvel that the masters of toilet technology and Nintendo, one of the leaders of technological innovation in the world, cannot come up with a better way to heat buildings than this. Come on. Most of the cool stuff the Japanese use during winter would not even be necessary if they had central heating, things like the heated toilet seat (which, I love of course), the hot carpet, the *kotatsu*. Using these things are strategies of the Japanese to keep away the cold. Taking long baths, eating *nabe* hot pot at night, drinking green tea. It is their way of coping with the cold.

Ultimately, I think it goes back to the Japanese spirit of *gaman*. Endurance. Whenever there is something they don't like or is tough, whether the pains of childbirth, the cold winters, unhappy marriage or an unfulfilling job, just *gaman*. Endure. Suck it up. Deal with it. No matter how you say it, the Japanese have mastered it. I love Japan so much, that I too, have learned to *gaman* the Japanese winters. Somehow, over the years, the cold has gotten a little less biting and the winter foods a little more delicious. I have even learned to *gaman* the frostbite I get on my toes during especially cold winters. I can *gaman* with the best of them, but I still don't understand why it is necessary for me to always be cold here. I probably never will. So, for now, when I am freezing and cannot bear it anymore, I will just go sit on the toilet.

#3

Views on Adoption

養子を迎えること
に対しての
考え方

My husband and I have been blessed with three beautiful daughters, but even before we had kids, we talked a lot about adoption and decided to pursue it at sometime in our lives if it was God's will for us. Our closest friends in Japan adopted two beautiful kids, and it was such a blessing to watch God knit the hearts of this international family together that, when our oldest daughter was six months old, we applied to a Christian adoption agency in Tokyo. We had heard there were not many babies available, so we prepared ourselves to wait for a couple of years, but okay with that since we had our hands full with our new daughter. Little did we know, our adoption journey would be full of potholes and detours, and that, six years later, we still wouldn't be at our destination.

Japanese people don't adopt. They don't think about adoption. They don't talk about adoption. They don't understand adoption. They don't adopt. Being from America, where every kind of imaginable family, including one formed through adoption, can be found, the Japanese apathy towards adoption puzzled me at first. After talking to friends and those in Japanese social services, I started to understand why adoption is so uncommon here.

1. Bloodlines = Family

Much more than in America, blood connection is crucial in Japan. The Japanese feel a strong connection and loyalty to family, and while they may be the most courteous, polite people in the world, love and loyalty is restricted to family. What is family? Although changing recently, family has always been defined in Japan by bloodlines. This can be seen most clearly in the family registry system (*koseki*). Every Japanese is entered into their family's registry at birth. They remain there until death or in the case of females, marriage. When a woman marries, she is erased from her family's registry and entered into her husband's, becoming legally only a member of his family. These registries are legally binding. Foreigners married to Japanese were not even

125

allowed onto their Japanese spouse's registry until July of last year. If they had either biological children or adopted ones, the children could only be on the Japanese spouse's registry or the foreign spouse's registry, not both.

Finally, last July, Japan introduced many sweeping immigration reforms to improve the lives of foreign residents. Giving foreigners equal access to family registries is huge progress for a country notoriously slow to make changes. Up until just fifteen years ago or so, foreigners were fingerprinted, and that fingerprint placed on their "alien registration card." Being fingerprinted and called an alien doesn't exactly make one feel welcome. But now, the fingerprinting is gone, along with the "alien card." Now it is just called a "residence card." To be sure, Japan has come a long way. Due to the new laws, international families are finally able to be joined together on the same family registry, making legal matters and documentation much simpler indeed. For me, more than anything, these changes just make me feel equal.

I have heard stories that some hospitals in the past have conducted under the table adoptions, made disturbingly simple by the family registry system. When a woman gives birth, one of the first things the hospital does is to write the mother's name on the official birth certificate. Legally, whoever's name is on this document is the legal mother of the baby. The mother then takes the certificate to the local city hall within ten days of birth and puts her baby into the family registry. In the case of an unwanted pregnancy leading to an under the table adoption, the hospital will put the name of the adoptive mother on the birth certificate, and that woman can go to city hall the same day to register that child as her own. Simple as that. This is illegal and immoral of course, but I hear it is sometimes still done today. Putting an unwanted child on a family registry is often very shameful for Japanese people, so they try to avoid shaming the family name at all costs.

2. Abortion

Abortion in Japan is not the hot-button issue it is in U.S. With a Christian population of less than 1%, and none of the Japanese religions offering much public condemnation of the practice, there are not nearly the moral implications of abortion as can be found in the West. In fact, abortions are performed at most maternity clinics by the same doctors and midwives who deliver babies later in the day. However, abortions are not covered by the national health care system.

Early in my third pregnancy, at about five weeks, I had bleeding and I was terrified I was miscarrying. My doctor told me it was too early to see the baby on ultrasound, so I had to wait a week or so to know whether or not I was still pregnant. I was on bed rest for that week, and while I was worried, I had a peace in my heart and nausea in my gut, so I was confident that things would be okay. I went in for an ultrasound at six weeks. The baby had a definite shape, even though only 5 mm in size. But can you believe that at six weeks and 5 mm, that baby had a heartbeat as strong as my own, beating clearly and powerfully through the monitor? It was one of the most moving experiences of my life. How could anyone hear that and think it wasn't a life?

Although Japan is not a particularly religious country, and most people see few moral implications regarding abortion, most Japanese women I know feel uncomfortable with it. My midwife friends without fail tell me that it is their least favorite work assignment, and they hate participating in abortions. Most women I know say they would not have an abortion. Of course, once she is confronted with an unwanted pregnancy, her response may be different, but most women I know feel uncomfortable with it. But ultimately, it is not always her choice. Even though she may not want to abort, she may be pressured by her boyfriend or family. Although shotgun weddings are becoming more and more acceptable in this socially conservative country, I have heard of cases where traditional parents who would be shamed by an illegitimate child put extreme pressure on their daughter to have an abortion. And because of the filial piety in the hearts of Japanese children, they are more likely to give in to the pressure than more independent, strong-willed Westerners.

The fact is, most unwanted pregnancies in Japan end in abortion, which means there are very few babies given up for adoption. Many women probably do not even consider it to be an option. When I taught about adoption in a culture class, many students told me that they had never thought about adoption, and many didn't even know it was possible in Japan. Of course, legally in Japan abortion is only allowed up to twelve weeks except in the case of medical necessity, so many women who discover pregnancy later than that have to consider options other than abortion. Many women will abort pregnancy later than that if they learn their babies have a disability or handicap. Many of the agencies in Japan who provide adoption services do so as a secondary ministry; their main work is counseling unwed mothers to choose life, and if they do so and cannot raise the baby themselves, they take charge of the baby to look for adoptive parents.

The most common type of adoption in Japan is actually adopting adults. This sounds strange to the Western ear, but if a family does not have a male heir, they will sometimes legally adopt a daughter's husband to carry on the family name. That man is erased from his family's registry and entered into his wife's, taking her name, family responsibilities and inheritance rights. Unlike adopting unrelated children, this practice is accepted in Japan as a necessary way to carry on the family name.

3. Ways of thinking

Many Japanese think the adoption of children leads to way too many problems. First of all, unlike in the West, most Japanese feel that children will not be happy with parents who are not their own. They think parents cannot possibly love an adopted child with the same intensity as a biological child. Many of my friends say they feel sorry for the child, because that child is not wanted by birth parents, and cannot be possibly loved fully by adoptive parents. They think the child will be devastated when he discovers the truth of his birth, realizing he is unloved by everyone (remember they think adoptive parents cannot fully love an adopted child). Adoption is a shameful thing to them, so the truth of it should be hidden from the child for as long as possible.

Most parents in the U.S. openly talk to their children about the fact they are adopted, many even celebrating "Gotcha Day," the day the child came to join the family. I have had numerous discussions and even arguments with Japanese people, with them trying to convince me that it is impossible for me to love an adopted child the same as my three biological children. They say that I may think I can love the child as my own, but that the adopted child won't think so; he or she will always feel second best. I strongly disagree, because I believe that family is formed through love, not blood, and that our love will make that adopted child feel fully loved and totally secure. Plenty of parents share blood with their kids, but do not have the right to be called parents.

My friends Rocky and Marla adopted two children-- Hana and Kai. Anytime someone tells me you cannot love adopted kids as your own, I just start talking about them. When I see them together, I see a real family. Not a family formed by blood, but through unconditional love. Marla was so committed to her daughter Hana, that she bought this funky contraption on the internet that allowed her to nurse Hana, even though she wasn't producing milk. It was more for bonding, but you know what? She started producing milk after a while even though she hadn't given birth. Impossible, you may say, but it's true. The love she had for that baby causes hormonal changes that allowed her to start lactating. Anyone want to tell me now that you can't fully love an adopted baby?

They love their kids, and their kids deeply love them back. I know that they feel totally secure in the love of their parents. Rocky and Marla talk openly with them about the fact they are adopted, telling them that God blessed them with two wonderful kids, that they are precious gifts from Him. They celebrate Gotcha Day every year. There are no secrets in this family, and it is a much, much healthier family than most I know. I once had them come to a class to talk about adoption because more than anything, I want the Japanese people to come to see adoption as the beautiful thing it is, and get rid of all the misconceptions and stereotypes they have about it. If they see Rocky and Marla and still decide adoption is not for them, that's fine. But I want them to acknowledge that their view of a person's ability to love is way too small, and I know that if they meet this cool family they will.

My friend, Marla, and her adopted son, Kai enjoying a good laugh.

Most of my Japanese friends can understand people who adopt because they are unable to have children. As rare as it is, desperate parents who have not had success with fertility treatment may turn to adoption as their last hope. However, while many people respect our desire to raise a Japanese baby, few of them can understand why we would want to adopt when we already have three beautiful, healthy girls. It makes absolutely no sense to them. Once, a friend even tried to talk me out of it. She said it would be too hard on the child. This was the first time anyone had ever tried to talk me out of adoption because they thought the child would be unhappy; up to that point, most objections had centered on our ability to love the child and treat him the same as our biological children. To many Japanese, even if I have 100% confidence that I can love that child as my own, the child will not think that I do.

4. Strong Parental Rights

Japanese parents very rarely relinquish parental rights, and Japanese courts even more rarely sever them. Most children in orphanages and social facilities have parents who cannot raise them, but they do not want other people to raise them either. I tend to see it as the epitome of selfishness. I am sure that it is a shameful thing that goes against the Japanese sense of responsibility for a stranger to raise your child, but I see it as children being denied a chance at happiness. That being said, because adoption is so rare here, even if they were available for adoption, the chance of them being adopted by a Japanese family is not too good. The foster parent system, with temporary, no-strings-attached, government supported childcare, is much more popular among the Japanese. Most foreigners, however, do not choose this option because they are afraid that one day the child will be taken away from them. In addition, many of them also may choose to one day return to their home country, and foster parents cannot take a foster child with them to live in another country.

The Japanese courts very rarely sever parental rights, even in the case of abuse. The courts may take the kids away from abusive parents, but those parents still have many decision-making powers in regards to the child. Until recently, parents of children in facilities could still receive the national childcare

131

allowance. This government support, calculated based on the ages and number of children in a family, is given to parents whose incomes fall under the salary cap to help with childrearing expenses. This is a significant amount of money. I receive about $1500 three times a year, an amount which helps a lot and for which I am thankful. The government intends this money to help offset childrearing expenses and help increase the birthrate, but birth parents of children in institutions were receiving this monthly stipend even though they were doing nothing to raise their children, hence had no financial expenses. Due to an outcry about the ridiculousness of the situation, in October 2011, parents of children in facilities in Japan became unable to receive the childrearing allowance.

My family's journey to adopt a Japanese baby started over six years ago with our application to a Christian adoption agency in Tokyo, which mainly deals with counseling women to choose life. We were told that childless couples would be prioritized, which we completely understood, and that there were very few babies available at the time. We are still waiting six years later. Thinking that we should explore other avenues, we thought about pursuing adoption through the Japanese government. Not knowing where to start, we went to the city office to ask about what steps we should take. They looked at us like we were crazy when we inquired about how to adopt. Five or so people huddled together trying to figure out what to do with this strange request from this crazy foreigner. Finally, they told us to call the Child Consultation Office. I did this, and was told that it was virtually impossible in Fukuoka Prefecture to adopt. They told me that I should go to Tokyo or Osaka, that it would be easier there. I was incredulous that in my city of over a million, and prefecture of five million, there were no adoptable children. Government adoption is a long process of interviews and visits with the child, and both Tokyo and Osaka are too far and too expensive for us to go through it. In addition, our second and third daughters were born soon after, so we temporarily put adoption on hold.

About a year ago, we decided to pursue adoption again. We wanted to add to our family, but we are getting older so instead of pregnancy we started thinking about adoption again. We could pursue an international adoption, which is much easier, but we have a strong heart to adopt and raise a Japanese child with our biological children. We love this country, so we want to love and raise a Japanese child. We contacted the Child Consultation Office again and set up an appointment. We were told that there are three ways to get a child—special adoption, foster-to-adopt, and temporary foster care. We were not interested in temporary foster care. The foster-to-adopt system provided children to you that would never go back to their birth parents, so there was little risk of the children being taken away. However, as mentioned before, there was no way we could ever return to the States and officially bring the child into our family using this route. The last route, special adoption, was the one that we wanted to take.

We were told, again, that there is not one adoptable child in the entire city of Kitakyushu, population one million. They told me that they average a whopping one adoption a year, and with five couples on the waiting list ahead of us, we should expect to wait five years or more. Wow. I was floored. What about all the thousands and thousands of kids in facilities? They are not adoptable, because the parents or the courts will not sever parental rights. These children are more or less trapped in these facilities until they are 18. The facilities provide for their material needs but they cannot provide the love these kids need; many of the kids are in those places due to abuse or neglect by birth parents who cannot take care of them or in some cases, do not want them. It is really a sad, heartbreaking situation.

There is a baby hatch at a hospital in Kumamoto Prefecture where parents who cannot raise a baby can leave the child in a safe place in secrecy, no questions asked. This was formed to try to protect children from being abandoned by desperate parents who felt like they had no options. In the first four years of operation, over 50 babies were left, but what to do with them is a problem because they have no paperwork, and there is always a chance the birth parents will return to claim the child. More than anything, Japanese authorities want to keep children with their birth parents whenever possible. This baby hatch has been very controversial in Japan because there are those who feel this opens a door for parents to shirk responsibility and take the easy way out. Others feel that it protects children that would have been abandoned had the baby hatch not been an option. I have always wondered what happens to these kids, but I suspect that they, too, are placed in institutions. The government is probably hoping against hope that the birth parents or another relative will come back for the child one day.

My family is still trying to figure out how to adopt. My girls love the idea. Just this morning, Mia thought adopting a baby would be a nice thing to do for Christmas; if only it were that easy! We are considering another Christian agency, which requires only travel and documentation costs for adoption. Being Christians, we would love to adopt through a Christian agency, because their vision and motivation is the same as ours: to love and rescue unloved children, and to show the people of Japan that we can love an adopted child fully and deeply with the love of Christ.

Our girls.

We had no idea when we began this journey six years ago that we would still be waiting and frustrated at this point. But we still feel called by God to adopt, and as long as He is calling us and there are still unloved kids who need to be loved, we will not give up. Somewhere out there is a beautiful child that God is knitting together just for us, a beautiful baby who will make our family complete.

#4

Tanshin Funin

単身赴任

I am hoping that most people reading this have no idea what *tanshin funin* is, and that it motivates them to keep reading. The reason that I kept this phrase in Japanese rather than translating it into English is simple: there is no English equivalent because most Western countries do not even have this concept. Intrigued? Begging and pleading to find out what I am talking about? Probably not begging, but maybe, interested? Translated directly, I think *tanshin funin* would be "for the primary breadwinner in a family, almost always the father, to live away from his family for an extended period of time for work." As you can see, while it is a simple two-word phrase in Japanese, it took me 25 words to explain sufficiently its meaning in English. The Chinese characters mean to be a single person to go somewhere for duty. Why do Japanese people choose to live like this, and what does it mean for family life?

First of all, work transfers are very common in Japanese society. Many employees are transferred every few years, and transfers are mandatory for most public officials, public school teachers and preschool teachers. No matter how much a worker may enjoy his current posting, or how much the people he is serving likes him, transfer is inevitable for the Japanese public servant. Not just that, most workers are not even informed of their transfers until the end of March, with their new post beginning in early April. My church has had many hastily planned farewell parties, with regular members standing up after worship informing us this is their last week. They have no time to say goodbye to family and friends, let alone pack up their stuff for a move. Many times, the length of the transfer is unknown, which may be one reason the father goes off by himself. However, the main reason, I think, is children.

In Japan, children are the center of family life and the center of society. Their well-being and emotional stability is of utmost importance. This can be seen from early on in infancy, when the mother begins to sleep with the new baby, often at the expense of time with her husband. Babies very rarely sleep through the night, because mothers rush to hold and nurse them at the first hint of a cry. I think some of my friends thought I was abusing my kids when I would let them cry it out while trying to get them on a schedule, but most of them respected my ways after they saw it worked and I was sleeping much more than they did.

Sometimes I think many new mothers lose their identity after having children. Many of them stop calling their husbands by their names and instead address him as *"Papa"* or *"Otoosan,"* the Japanese equivalents of Daddy or Father. They spend time with their *mamatomo*, short for *mama tomodachi* (their children's friends' mothers), often not being called by their names, but rather "Keita's mommy" or "Haruka's mommy." Of course, even in America we say to our kids stuff like, "Ask Luke's mommy if you can come over." I am not talking about being addressed like this. In Japanese mommy circles, "Mia's mommy" is used in place of a name, like "Mia's mommy, can I talk to you for a second?" I must admit that I really dislike this. Before I had kids, my name was Anne, and who I am has not changed. I am still Anne, and I would smack Riz up side the head if he ever started calling me "Mommy" instead of "Honey" as he has always called me.

Other friends seem to stop doing things they used to do and pour all their energy, time and effort into their children. Of course, I realize that when you become a parent sacrifice is inevitable; your children need you. Not just you providing food, clothing and shelter. They need you. They need your attention. They need your time. But I don't think that necessitates giving up your identity, what it is to be you. In fact, your children can benefit more from you being you than from you losing your identity. I am Anne to my American friends, Anne Sensei to my students, Anne-chan to my Japanese friends, and Honey to Riz. I am Mommy to Mia, Abby and Emmy, but not to anyone else, so I would rather people here just call me Anne-chan. Most of the people around me are catching on, and I am hearing my name called more and more lately. I like that.

So, children are the center of the family, and education is at the center of a child's life. When a father is transferred for work, for a child to be uprooted from his school and friends, perhaps disrupting test studies and causing emotional distress, is not an option. In most cases, the mother will stay behind in the family's home with the children. The father will rent an apartment or stay in company housing during his time of transfer, which is sometimes indefinite.

The thing that bothers me most about this is that I think keeping a family together is more important than anything, something that should be strived for at all costs. In Japan, of course, family relationships are important, but my impression is that work and children's stability trump keeping a family together. Many times when work and family obligations collide, work prevails. Whether it is because I am an American or a Christian or maybe both, this is something I have a really hard time accepting. For me, I work to honor God, serve my students, and provide for my family, but my family is much more important to me, and I would sacrifice work if ever made to choose. But in the Japanese culture, that is sometimes not an option. I get the sense that even if a father doesn't want to live away from his family or put work first, he has no choice. The societal expectations about work dictate his behavior. Many Japanese businessmen work late into the night, and on the weekends. In addition to regular work duties, they also have regular drinking parties that keep them away from dinnertime with family. I have a friend who once told me that she would love to have another baby, but it is too hard being a single mother. She isn't technically a single mother, but she feels that way. Her husband goes to work before their daughter wakes up, gets home after she is in bed, and even works on Saturdays. The only time he sees his daughter's face in on Sunday. I have met this father and he is a nice guy and really loves his daughter. But how sad is this? He only sees her one day a week?

Translation: "I hardly ever see you, Dad, but I love you and you're really important to me."

I remember once on Father's Day at the local bakery, children received a free ice cream if they drew a picture of their father and brought it in to the bakery. I was saddened to see a picture of one father with the following message: "I hardly ever see you Dad, but you are really important to me." It broke my heart to read that.

Five years ago, my older brother was transferred to his company's Tokyo office for a three-year term. It was never even an option for him to come by himself. He saw this as an amazing cultural experience for his entire family, and his wife felt the same way. I know my brother loves his family passionately, and he would have been miserable without them. I know his wife and children would have felt the same way. Of course I am not saying that Japanese people love their families less than Americans do, I just wonder if there is less thought given to emotional attachment and more to practicality. It is more practical to keep kids in a familiar environment so they can do well. The mother may have a hard time and the father may be lonely, but everyone just has to *gaman* for the sake of the family. Just like the Japanese *gaman* the cold, they likewise *gaman* being separated from their families, mainly because they do not think they have a choice. If I had a nickel for every time I hear the work *gaman* in daily conversation, I would be a rich woman. As an American, I could never *gaman* having my husband away from me for work for an extended period of time. Totally apart from the help he gives me with the kids and housework, his very presence in the home calms me and gives me peace. I know everything will be okay with him around.

Last March, he went to Las Vegas for a photography convention for ten days. He has gone many times, and as much as I hate it, I know it's a valuable time for him as a photographer. Besides, there are many people who help me out while he is gone, and it was Spring Break, so work was not very busy. This time was a little different from previous years, though. My kids' Japanese grandma, Ito Baba was out of town visiting her daughter, so she could not help me. Junko was helping her sick father-in-law in the hospital, so she could not help either. I figured as long as everyone stayed healthy, I would be okay. Yeah, right.

Two days before Riz left, my two youngest kids got ear infections, and were grumpy for days after. We had to take Abby to the emergency room in the middle of the night because the pain was so bad. We were turned away from the hospital closest to our house because there was no ENT on call, so we called the emergency call center, and were told there is no emergency ENT in the entire city. You gotta be kidding me. What do you do with an emergency earache? Three guesses? That's right! *Gaman!* We called a hospital with emergency pediatrics, and they said, well, they could see her, but couldn't really give her antibiotics. She would have to visit an ENT the next day. Couldn't we just give her some painkiller and have her *gaman* until morning? Have you ever tried to reason with a screaming 4-year old that it would be very helpful if she could possibly *gaman* until morning? Mommy would really appreciate it. No *gaman*-ing going on here. My husband took her in to the ER, she got some painkillers, and she calmed down. The crisis had passed. For now.

Wednesday afternoon, Riz departed, and I went to work. Wednesday passed uneventfully. I woke up Thursday morning feeling a little cruddy, but figured I was just tired. I took the kids to school, went to work, and felt a headache and cough coming on. But in a common display of lack of common sense, which often occurs when it comes to me and exercise, I went jogging on the treadmill at work anyway. Stupid move. I felt worse. I realized that I had missed a call around lunch from the kids' school, which always means someone is sick. Sure enough, when I called back, I was told that it seemed my youngest, two-year-old Emmy, had come down with the chicken pox. The chicken pox. I knew it was a relatively harmless disease that most kids get in Japan (usually Japanese kids aren't vaccinated because parents don't want to pay 100 bucks; I just never got around to it!). But one thing I did know was what I hate almost as much as the cold--quarantine. I knew that chicken pox was extremely contagious and that Emmy would be banned from school until her doctor cleared her. Not only would that mean I had to take time off, but I would also have to entertain her at home for a week, no easy task. But due to unforeseen events, this wasn't really necessary. I ended up taking my contagious, disease-infected kid out to crowded public places every day.

On the way home from work, I crashed my car into the wall in my driveway while backing in. I had done that several times before and our car is old so I didn't even bother to look at the damage until later. Then, I picked Emmy up at school (after running over a construction cone at the preschool and crushing it!) a little after three and took her to the doctor. At this point, I had taken my temperature and decided I must have the flu. I never get a fever unless I have the flu, strep throat or a sinus infection, and the flu was going around. Since I had a highly contagious Emmy, I knew that I couldn't go to the doctor to get tested and get medicine. So I asked Emmy's pediatrician if he could test me. Why not? He made my chart, tested me (it was positive), and quarantined both of us. The pharmacy even brought us medicine over so we wouldn't infect other patients.

We went to get the other two girls after we finished at the pediatrician. We were told that since I had the flu, I couldn't go inside the preschool, so I waited outside while a teacher brought my girls out. We went home and the girls watched TV while I slaved in the kitchen over instant noodles. Feeling feverish, I had bought stuff to make the girls' favorite dish, cream stew, but had no energy to do it, so I decided to give them instant noodles. Just for the record, I had never bought cup noodles before for my kids, but I knew they liked noodles, so I figured it would be a winner.

What happened next is a little fuzzy, a pretty common occurrence in an emergency. The girls were watching their favorite Disney show and not paying much attention to anything else. I hear this is pretty typical behavior of most in the little people population. My kids watched way too much TV while Riz was gone. It is such an evil little invention killing brain cells, yet it entertains kids happily while parents are trying to make dinner or feel like death warmed over. I have a love-hate relationship with that little tube. There are days I want to throw it out the window, and others it is responsible for me keeping my sanity.

I heated up some water in my T-fal hotpot, and placed the noodles on the table to cool. Mia asked me if she could have her noodles a few minutes later, though I am not sure exactly how much later. The next thing I know she is screaming hysterically, lying on the floor. She had spilled the steaming hot noodles on her right calf, and since she only had on tights, they had not protected her leg at all. I had no experience with burns and had no idea what to do. I told her to hurry to the bathroom, but she couldn't walk. I pick her up, and carried her to the sink to put it under cold water, but she freaked out and I couldn't do it. I got an ice pack from the freezer, wrapped it in a towel and held her tight. I was panicking, she was hysterical, and my mind was racing trying to figure out what to do. I couldn't take her to the ER because Emmy and I were sick, and honestly, I have a terrible sense of direction and didn't think I could get there. Our Japanese grandma was out of town; our other church friends were busy. I couldn't call an ambulance because I couldn't take all the girls with me. I had no experience with burns and did not know how bad it was, but it was really red and the skin was peeling off over a pretty wide area. Finally, I decided to call my friend, Chie, who lived in the neighborhood.

Chie and I met just last year, but have become really close lately. She also has three daughters about the ages of my own, so we go through a lot of the same stuff at the same time. She rushed over and tried to calm down a screaming Mia. She thought it was pretty bad and that Mia should go to the hospital, but Mia was screaming that she wouldn't go, that she just wanted to get medicine. Chie tried to reason with her and tell her that we didn't know what kind of medicine she needed unless we went to the hospital. Mia was still hysterical, and finally, after Chie got Mia to talk to the medical operator who assured her the doctor wouldn't hurt her, she agreed to go to the hospital. I cannot tell you how moved I was that Chie left her three young daughters at home alone eating dinner for two hours in order to take Mia to the ER for me. That is a true friend.

After they left, I tried to calm down and take care of my other two daughters. I called Riz in Vegas. I had just gotten off the phone with him before Mia's accident, so I worried him by calling again so soon. I was crying while telling him what happened, crying out of worry, exhaustion, and of course, guilt. Why had I let Mia take the noodles so soon? I should have made sure that they were not so hot. I should have made her eat them at the table. I should have watched her better. The list of what ifs went on and on. I was sobbing while talking to Riz, just overwhelmed with all that was going on without my man beside me to help. How do single mothers do it? What do they do when stuff like this happens? I respect them more than ever now, after this nightmarish ten days away from my husband.

Chie and Mia returned two hours later. Mia had a huge bandage over her 2nd degree leg burns. The doctor said that Mia would have to return the following day, and that her burns were pretty deep. They would not know until later if the burns would leave scarring or not. She seemed to be okay, not in any pain and just really hungry when she got home. I let her sleep with me that night because I was so guilt-ridden and so worried about her.

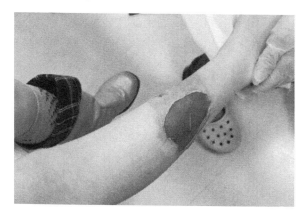

Mia's burn the day after.

The next day, the girls Japanese granddad, Ito-Jiji, took us to the hospital. For the record, he crashed the car for the third time in two days, running into the same wall in my driveway! Anyway, we arrived at the hospital for our appointment with the reconstructive surgeon. Mia's burn was severe enough to have to be treated by a burn specialist, not a regular dermatologist. I wasn't prepared for how bad the burn was. There was a huge raw area on her calf, surrounded by a band of dead, black skin around the wound. It looked awful, but she didn't seem to be in too much pain. I found out that we were going to be visiting the hospital every day for a while to get her bandage changed. For more than a week, it week, it produced pus so the wound had to be sterilized and the bandage changed.

After returning from the hospital that day, I found out about a serious problem at work that I had to take care of. So, I had to take my flu-riddled self (although the medicine I took made me feel much better), my daughter with chicken pox, and my second-degree burn inflicted daughter to the office with me, the last place I really wanted to go that day. But like a good Japanese, I tapped into the *gaman* spirit and got things taken care of.

The rest of the week was a blur. I took Mia to the doctor for her burn everyday. I would drop off Abby at school, take Mia to the doctor, take Mia to school, take Emmy to work with me, and then pick up Mia and Abby around dinnertime. Because of my horrible sense of direction, and the incredible sympathy of friends, someone drove us to the hospital everyday. This meant I could leave the sick kids in the car, and take the healthy ones to school. Abby was the only healthy one, but she was going through a lot of emotional stuff, probably the result of Riz being gone and all the attention going to her sisters. She started peeing in her pants; she talked back to me; once, she even kicked Mia in the leg on purpose. This was not the Abby I was used to. The kids always have a hard time emotionally when Riz is gone. They get needy and all want me to hold them all the time, but this time was worse than usual. In addition to all the physical problems, I was dealing with neediness, clinginess, incessant sibling bickering, and whining. This in turn made me grumpy and snappy towards my kids. I was reaching my limit. This was all going on while I was trying to recover from the flu. I had not rested at all since being tested, and I was running on fumes.

If it had not been for the incredible help and support of my friends, I don't think I could have made it. Since our regular line of support was not available, other friends and church members stepped in as pinch hitters. One friend made dinner Friday night, another Saturday lunch. My student came by Saturday night unannounced and made dinner for our whole family. People prayed for us, supported us, and that is what got us through. Times like that remind me how hard it is not having my mother around to help. This is probably one of my biggest struggles about living in Japan. No matter how old I get, I still need my mommy.

Anyway, Riz made it back to Japan the following Friday. That Wednesday, all three girls finally went to school, and I went to work by myself for the first time in a week. I thought I was over the hump, until Abby woke up at 6 am the following morning throwing up. Wonderful, I thought. It just wouldn't be complete until they were all sick. She stayed home, got medicine, and seemed fine by lunchtime. The following day they all went to school again, and I picked them up early to go to our cafe at church. Riz was coming home that night, so I knew that whatever happened today, everything would be okay.

Abby, who had been fine all day, said her tummy hurt and then, preceded to puke all over the back of the sanctuary. After uttering endless apologies, I took the girls home and left the staff to clean up the mess. Abby felt better, as most people do after a good hurl, so she relaxed on the sofa while I prepared dinner for the other two kids. Actually, preparing dinner just meant heating up some stew that Junko had made for us. Riz was coming home in a few hours, so I wanted to look nice for him, clean up the place, and have everything perfect when he came home. I had on my favorite clothes, the house was clean, and I was relaxed. Then, ten minutes before Riz came home, Emmy, my youngest, threw up everywhere. I mean everywhere. How could such a little creature produce such an incredible amount of throw up? And she was in the worst possible place for it. Sitting on our vinyl sofa, her vomit seeped between the cushions, spewed all over the carpet, all over Emmy, all over me. I didn't know what to do first, so Emmy and I jumped in the shower and put on our pajamas. I cleared the kids out of the living room, put on a mask and gloves, and went to work cleaning up the mess. I used antibacterial wipes and sprayed *Febreeze* everywhere, but I couldn't get rid of the smell.

Riz came home just as I was finishing up, so instead of me looking pretty waiting for him to come home in my spotless living room, I was wearing my pajamas, a mask and gloves, and the whole room smelled like puke. Welcome home, honey! I cannot tell you how relieved I was to see him come through the door. My man was home so all was right with the world. The kids were bouncing off the walls with excitement. Mia just kept screaming, "Daddy! Daddy!" It was great. The worst week of my life was over.

Riz (far right) celebrating with other international award-winning photographers.

The reason I went on such an incredibly long tangent about the worst week of my life is this: I was a total useless mess after just ten days without my husband. I am a mess sometimes even when things don't go poorly. I need him. He brings peace to my heart and stability to my life. I could never live away from my husband, nor would I ever want to. One thing that disturbs me about Japanese families is that many wives don't mind their husbands living away from them, and some of them actually seem to like it. It is almost like they get used to doing things alone, and when their husband is around he throws a wrench in things and messes up the routine. Many of them resign themselves to it because they figure it is just the way things work in Japan. Still, many of my friends, whom I know love their husbands, just don't seem to be a mess without their husbands like I am a mess without mine. Maybe they are stronger than I am? I am not convinced that being okay on your own without you husband is a good thing. I think God created us to need each other, and to be better together than on our own.

Of course, all people should be able to function when circumstances force them to be away from their spouses for a certain period of time. I have so much respect for military wives who are apart from their husbands for six months to a year. How do they do it? They don't have a choice, so I guess they have to learn to *gaman,* too. I guess in some ways, *tanshin funin* is like this. The difference is, deployments are for a limited time, most couples hate being apart, and cannot wait to get together again. When a military member is transferred, they will almost always go with their families. So in this way, it is totally different from *tanshin funin.*

Japanese men work for their families, but at what cost? Their long hours and time apart from their families provide a nice house, good education, and nice stuff for their families, but I think kids just want to see their fathers. Just like the kid at the bakery who drew the picture about his dad which said, "I hardly ever see you, Dad, but I love you and you are really important to me." Children need their parents to be emotionally stable. I think that means having both parents with them as much as possible. Some people may say that this is just a cultural difference, but I am not convinced of that. To me, keeping family together is central to not only happy, flourishing children, but to a happy society. *Tanshin funin* drives me crazy.

#5

The Education System

教育制度

I remember the first time I really thought the education system in Japan was crazy. I was in my second year in Japan, riding the train home from work one day. Sitting on the seat across from me was a student, probably middle school age, looking totally exhausted. He could not stay awake no matter how hard he tried. He would doze off, bang his head against the wall behind him or the handrail in front on him, wake up and fall immediately back to sleep. He was wiped out. He had bags under his eyes. I am sure from the exhaustion he was one of the most pitied creatures on earth, the *jukensei*, or, student studying for entrance exams.

A student's final year of middle school and high school is not fun, as they must spend hours after getting home from a long day at school studying on their own for entrance exams for the high school or university of their dreams, or going to cram school for extra study several times a week. For a *jukensei*, life stops. Those involved in extracurricular activities at school retire (I am not kidding. This is the word they use in Japanese). Life becomes about study. Mothers have it bad, too. They must work hard to ensure success for their children by preparing nutritious meals, giving necessary encouragement and prodding, and providing a peaceful study environment. If the student fails, it reflects badly not only upon the child, but upon the mother, too.

There are two systems in particular that I think make the education system here displeasing to me: entrance exams and cram schools, neither of which we have to a comparable degree in the United States. Of course, we have the SAT and ACT tests, but the results of those tests do not control the future of students like they do in Japan. If a student does poorly on the SAT, he can just take it again and again. In the event he still cannot get a good enough score to get into his first choice, there is always another less prestigious university he can go to. There is also the option of going to community college for a year or two, then transferring, which is much easier than initial entrance. In Japan, students generally start preparing for these exams about a year before the exam period. There are two main university entrance exams in Japan. The first is the Center Test, which is similar to the SAT but consists of five or more subjects. This is a unified national exam that is given only once a year, on the same day, all over the country. In addition, each university has its own entrance exam, which applicants must also take. There is also a recommendation system; lucky students put forward on recommendation by high school teachers have an interview and take a much easier exam. While admission through this system is not guaranteed it is much easier and much less stressful to get in this way.

The entrance exams are so important for the future of students that they quit doing pretty much everything but studying. Students who fail the entrance exams to the university of their choice can either go to another university, or become a *ronin*. A *ronin* actually means "masterless samurai," but in today's Japan it refers to students who enter a preparatory school or study on their own after failing to enter the university of their choice. They attend this school full-time, sometimes living in the dorms, to get the extra instruction needed to pass the exams next time around. Students who really want to enter medical school often become *ronin*, but students wishing to study in all fields can be found in these special preparatory schools. Tuition is pricey, but parents are willing to cover it because so much is at stake.

So, once students do get into university, they can breathe a sigh of relief. Many Americans have a stereotype that Japanese university students just party all the time; they think students are so stressed out and work so hard to get in to university, that once they do, they don't do anything. While this may be true of some liberal arts universities, students in science and medical schools are very committed to their studies. Of course, they party and drink just like university students all over the world, but the stereotype that they do not even have to come to class to graduate is definitely not true. I do think that it is a time of freedom for them, a respite between the stress of studying for entrance exams and the stress of job hunting and beginning to work in society.

In the past, once students started working, they rarely changed jobs. That first job became a lifetime career. But the system of lifetime employment is disappearing, and it is not uncommon for more individualistic Japanese students to quit a job he or she does not like and find another one, often doing a year of working holiday in a foreign country in between. Recently, many young people are rebelling against the system to an even greater extent, choosing to be a *freeta* or a NEET. A *freeta* is generally a young person who floats around doing different part-time jobs, usually living at home. He wants freedom from the constraints and pressure of a full-time job, and doesn't value money as much as time to pursue his hobbies and interests. A NEET (Not In Education, Employment, or Training) is more extreme. This young person pretty much stays at home and leeches off his parents, doing nothing, as the name NEET would suggest.

Many students who do choose to enter university must not only decide their school but also major at the time of admission. They first take the university's entrance exam, and then the exam for the department they want to enter. At most U.S. universities, like mine in Virginia, all students take general education courses their first three semesters, and then declare a major second semester of sophomore year. At that point, many students have a clearer idea of what they like and what they may want to pursue as a career. Of course, many still don't know. They just major in psychology or some other major that is relatively useless without graduate school. For me, the useless-without-grad-school major of choice was religion. I had no idea what career I would pursue with it, but I loved it, and religion classes seemed to be the only ones I could get good grades in. My GPA was abysmal my freshman year and sophomore years; I even failed a math class because I couldn't figure out how to use a graphing calculator. But suddenly, because I was studying something I loved, my GPA magically inflated.

Personally, I don't think there is anything wrong with pursuing studies you like in college without really knowing what you want to do as a career. I think it would be pretty miserable to study something you are not gifted in or not interested in just because the field will pay well after college. Chances are, if you don't like studying it in college, you won't like working at it after. So, I majored in religion, excelled in my studies and graduated with honors. I went on a missions trip to China and spent a year in seminary. Then, in a whirlwind romance, my husband swept me off my feet. We fell madly in love, and got engaged five weeks later. Since Riz had been hired by the Japanese government to teach in a high school there, I figured I would tag along. I actually had wanted to move to China, but my hillbilly self figured Japan was close enough. Imagine the conversation I had with my Mom. I don't remember it all that well, but I imagine it went something like, "Um, Mom? I am dropping out of seminary, getting married and moving to Japan. Cool?" It wasn't really cool, but she loves me so she eventually got over it.

After three years in Japan, I came back to the U.S. when I was 27 and still did not know what I wanted to do with my life. I finally figured it out that year, when I realized how much I enjoyed teaching English to teenage Japanese students. I had been tutoring a Japanese high school exchange student, and I loved it. In my first stint in Japan, I taught English to little kids, which had been fun but was not my calling. I soon enrolled in grad school, got my M.A. in Applied Linguistics, and was off to teach in Japan soon after graduation. My husband, constant support that he is, came along even though he didn't have a job or a clue of what he would do. He wanted me to follow my dream. Finally, nine years after entering college, I finally figured out what I wanted to do. So you can see why I have some sympathy for 18-year old students having to make decisions that will affect the rest of their lives at such a young age.

In addition to my objection that one test can determine a student's future, the way I see it, the entrance exam system promotes rote learning and memorization of facts and data. Students are expected to memorize a massive amount of information for the exams, and often say they just forget it after the test. There is of course, a time and a place for rote learning, and it does have value; I just feel like it is the main education approach in Japan. Many Japanese students are good test takers, but have not learned adequately how to express creativity, original thinking, or their opinions on a variety of subjects. Of course, I do not blame the students, but the system that created them. I think students need to be taught study and learning skills, not just taught to cram information into their heads. That way, they will have the ability to learn, teach themselves, retain what they learn and apply it to life. The inability to express an opinion is one of my biggest problems with education in Japan, and one reason I wish I could send my kids to international school, or even homeschool them. More than anything, I want them to learn to think for themselves, and question everything, not just blindly accept everything they are taught. I want them to learn independence and to be strong. I am starting them at a young age, by doing little things like telling them to get their own milk, and no, I will not go upstairs to get their pajamas. Maybe Japanese parents think I am being harsh, and maybe sometimes I am really just being a little lazy, but I want them to learn to do things for themselves, be it big things like pondering the meaning of life, or small things like getting their own milk.

Most Japanese classes are lecture-based, so students just take in information, and have little opportunity to express their opinions or question what they learn. Even if they want to, there is so much pressure just to get ready for the exams, they do not have the luxury or the time to really think about what they are learning. Many times, because teachers are so respected in Japan, they will just take what the teacher says as truth and not really question it. I read a story on the Internet recently that illustrates how many

Japanese will follow what they are told with little questioning. Three Japanese tourists in Australia drove right into the Pacific Ocean because their GPS told them that was the way. A funny story, maybe, but it is a good example of the Japanese character to follow authority. Teachers are the authority, and students are expected to listen to the teacher for the best results. That scares me, because I don't want that kind of power. Although I am well trained and confident that what I am teaching is correct most of the time, I know that I am human and make mistakes just like everyone else. I would love it if my students would question the accuracy of what I teach them. That would really make my day.

This high status of the teacher leads to incredible pressure and stress, especially for public school teachers. Teachers in Japan are responsible not only for the academic training and preparation of students (which would be stressful enough by itself), but for their moral growth and development as well. There have been cases when students are caught shoplifting or engaging in other deviant behavior, and the school is contacted before the parents. Why? Because the school is responsible for the moral education of the child. Bullying is a big problem in Japanese schools, and stopping bullying is considered the full responsibility of the teaching staff, in particular the principal of the school. A few years ago, a student committed suicide after being bullied, and several months later, the school principal committed suicide because he either felt responsible for the student's death, or the parents and community held him responsible for the death. Maybe both.

Japanese teachers do not just teach. They morally guide the students. They are responsible for home visits to each student in their homeroom. They often stay late everyday directing an after school club or activity, and are often gone on the weekends participating in competitions or games with these groups. There is not really a summer vacation, as teachers are expected at school everyday to prepare for the new term, attend meetings, and direct clubs and activities. Many Japanese public school teachers work hours comparable to Japanese businessmen, coming home late every night.

Nervous breakdowns are not uncommon, and seen as just part of the culture. I remember once asking about a teacher and being told, "Oh yeah, she had a breakdown. She will be back next year." I remember being flabbergasted in the offhand way this was relayed to me. It was almost like, "Yeah, she is honeymooning in Hawaii." I have never in my life heard of a public school teacher in the U.S. having a nervous breakdown from overwork or pressure. Work in Japan can be so stressful that they even have a word for working themselves to death, *karoshi*. Literally, it means 'dying from overwork.' My mom was a public school teacher most of her life, and very committed to her job and to her students. Yet, she was home by 4 pm almost everyday, and never worked in the summers. Sure, she brought papers home to grade, and sold tickets at basketball games every now and then, but it was never all that stressful as far as I could tell. The most complaining I ever heard was about the smart aleck attitudes of the students and the vulgar t-shirts.

There is much to be said for the commitment that Japanese public school teachers have to their jobs and their students. I am not sure if they are so committed because they really want to be, or because it is expected of them. It is probably a little of both. Japanese teachers pour their hearts into their students, but sometimes I wonder if this commitment comes at the cost of their own families. One of my friends is a public school teacher, as is her husband. He is in charge of a sports club at the school. The team is very strong, and he is always off somewhere with the team. He is home late everyday, and is gone almost every weekend. I have talked to his wife, and I know that she resents it and wishes he were home more. But, she takes the Japanese *"sho ga nai"* stance, which literally means, "It can't be helped." This is the way things work in Japan, and no matter now much she dislikes it, there is nothing to do but grin and bear it. *Gaman.*

The other thing I really dislike about the Japanese education system is the existence of cram schools. These special schools are full of students who study one to five times a week after their regular school classes are finished. Most students (or more likely their parents!) think that this extra study is the only way they can get ahead and get into the high school or university of their choice, thus assuring a successful future. I think the existence of these schools shows that the government is failing in providing an adequate education. It is the government's responsibility to provide the education the students need, and it is grossly unfair if a student who has the financial ability to pay for this extra instruction can get ahead because the government has failed to provide sufficient instruction to prepare students for university. I also feel that kids need balance. Kids need to play and relax and have fun. Isn't going to school all day long, and doing homework at night enough?

Not all Japanese students attend cram school. Many less ambitious students who stay close to home and attend local universities don't go to cram school. I have also heard of students who have gotten into prestigious universities without it. But this is the exception, not the rule. Most highly motivated students with dreams of attending high-level high schools and universities will go to cram school. The majority of students I have talked to see it as a kind of necessary evil. They don't love it or enjoy it, but it does help them to get where they want to go.

I am a laid back American with two main philosophies about childhood: it should be fun, and there should be a lot of family time. Of course education and learning is important, but there is so much more to life and to childhood. In fact, I think the term "education" has a broader meaning than it is given in Japan. Taking my kids to the zoo or reading books at home is education to me. I consider myself to have a successful career, and I thoroughly enjoyed my childhood. I studied hard, but I also played sports all the time, played outside after school, watched TV and took family vacations. One of my biggest criticisms of Japan is the lack of moderation I see in everything. They study too much. They work too hard. Sometimes, they even play too hard.

The local neighborhood sandlot baseball team practices two hours on Tuesday night, and every single Saturday, Sunday, and holiday from 8 am to 4 pm. These are elementary school kids, not high schools kids! This rigorous practice schedule leaves little time for family time. Baseball is the biggest time sucker of all in Japan. I once asked two college students who played baseball throughout high school if they ever took a family vacation. It seemed to me kind of impossible with the practice schedule most teams have. They told me that, no, they had never taken a family vacation. Never. Not even once. Sports and activities demand total commitment, just like studying. No wonder preschool students can be so undisciplined and university students party so much: these are the only two times in life they are pressure-free.

While it may seem that I don't like anything about the Japanese education system, that is not the case. I think the Japanese elementary school system is genius. It is relatively laid back. There are no uniforms, students seems to enjoy their studies, there is not too much homework, and kids have lots of time to play outside at recess. It is during these six years that students learn most of the Chinese characters (*kanji*) necessary to function in daily life. Gaijin like me, who start learning as adults, are pretty much fighting a losing battle. You see, you need to know at last 2000 *kanji* to be a literate member of Japanese society. Each of those *kanji* can have up to ten or so different readings, depending on the other *kanji* it is paired with. I have passed the hardest Japanese proficiency test for foreigners, and know many more *kanji* than most of my friends, yet I am still probably only at a junior high school literacy level. That, after studying for years and years. So, through attending a Japanese elementary school, my children can hopefully avoid the *kanji* struggles I have had. The math education system is also years ahead of the U.S.

The school meals are healthy, cheap and required: students are not allowed to bring their own lunches, and there is no choice about the menu. Every student in the city eats the same thing on the same day. If you don't like it, it's too bad. One of my friends hates curry, and complained that it was curry, curry, curry in Japanese school lunches. Curry and rice. Curry noodles. Curry chicken. But I think making kids all eat the same thing is a good thing because it exposes them to a wide variety of foods and keeps them from becoming picky eaters. When I was a kid, the school lunches in elementary school were balanced, but I have no memory of them tasting good. Mia genuinely likes the food, and comes home most everyday talking about how good it was, although kind of weird. They have almonds and tofu with fish and milk sometimes. Seems like a weird combination to me. Most Japanese will tell you that milk doesn't go all that well with traditional Japanese food, but it is a staple of the school lunch system, one of the remnants of the American influence from the period after WWII. Once, I attended a lecture on school lunches at Mia's school, and at the end we were served the same lunch the kids were eating that day for the grand total of $2.50. It was really good, and many of the parents weren't shy to ask for seconds.

Mia dancing at her elementary school sports festival.

Not only are school lunches healthy, but students are also responsible for serving them, and cleaning up afterwards. In addition, they must clean their classroom at the end of everyday. These responsibilities lead the students to take better care of the environment around them. Physical education is also important, with much time being spent in gym class and swimming. I was really surprised there was a swimming pool at the school, and that kids are taught basic swimming skills as part of the curriculum.

My oldest daughter, Mia, started elementary school last year, so I feel like I am still learning the ropes. The memory of the orientation we had two months before school started is still fresh in my mind. I came home with a thick packet of information and a panicking heart. Because I had gotten used to life in Japan after twelve years, I hadn't had that overwhelmed-I-have-absolutely-no-idea- what-I-am-doing feeling in a really long time. But this was new territory for me, and I knew that I was going to have to rely on Chie, whose middle daughter was in Mia's class. Since she has a third grader, too, she is used to it all and knows the system. Most of the other first-time elementary school mommies seemed just as overwhelmed as I was. Now, nine months later, I am getting in the flow, but I still can't believe how much paperwork comes home with her everyday. I forget to do something every now and then, but something always works out. That is my mantra for living in Japan: something will work out. The Japanese say, *nantoka naru*. I try to remember this anytime I get stressed. *Nantoka naru*.

But the month leading up to her entrance into elementary school, it was tough to remember my life mantra. I pulled out that orientation information tome and tried to maneuver the maze of all the stuff I had to do and buy. The list of stuff she needed was about a mile and a half long, starting with a $300 backpack called a *randoseru*.

Yes, I said a $300 backpack. The *randoseru*, from the Dutch word "ransel" is the symbol of Japanese elementary schools.

Technically, you don't have to buy it but everybody does. This backpack is made of a strong and durable leather, and designed to withstand the wear and tear of six years of elementary school. Of course, you can get them for as cheap as $100, but they are small, and larger A4 size files have to be bent to fit inside. God forbid that happening. The really cute colors like the ten different shades of pink demand top dollar, as do the ones with cute little hearts or stars on them. That is at least another fifty bucks or so. There is even a *randoseru* designed by NASA with some kind of ultra-durable space material or something. This one fetches top dollar, around $500. We dreaded the cost, but hit my mom up for $100 to help us out, telling her it was Japanese tradition for the grandmother to buy the *randoseru*, which is true. My mom said, "Fine, but make sure you hit up the other grandmother for Abby!"

I guess I can rationalize spending $300 on a backpack when I think she will use it for six years. If we bought a new backpack every year for $25 or so, six years of elementary school would cost $150. We opted for the mid-range *randoseru* because of course, it had to be pink, and the $100 ones did look pretty small. But at $300, I am glad I have two years to save for Abby's.

Some of the other school supplies I *could* buy through the school, some of it I *had* to buy through the school, and some of it, I was better off hitting the 100 yen shop or some cheap discount store. I just followed Chie's lead and did what she did. A week before school started I went shopping to make sure she had everything. I bet I had to buy 50 different things to prepare for elementary school. She even needed a harmonica, pianica hose, and I love this one, her own personal rag to clean the school with. My super mommy friends make these from old towels, even though you can buy two for a hundred yen at the 100 yen shop. If you ever want to feel bad about yourself, hang around with super mommies who make everything for their kids, including of course, embroidering their names on everything. No cheap 100 yen shop labels for them. These are the same mommies who make super *bentos.* They are great friends, very humble, and don't think that what they are doing is special. Granted they have a lot more time on their hands than I do, and personally, I have no regrets. I would rather spend my time playing with my kids than making homemade rags for them. I really respect my super mommy friends, but it just isn't me. I do wish, however, that I had more of their love for cooking and *bento* making. My kids are getting to be an age when they are going to be aware that their mommy's cooking is not quite as yummy as school lunches or their friends' mommies' *bentos.* Of course, my kids love me, and won't hold it against me (I hope!). Just the other day, Mia tried to convince me that my omelet and rice dish was much better than the one we had for dinner at a specialty restaurant. Personally, I thought she was nuts, but I was moved by her devotion to mommy.

So, after buying everything, including the two-for-one hundred yen rags, I sat down to write Mia's name on everything. Maybe you are saying, "Oh, I had to do that when my daughter was in preschool. It took over an hour!" Oh, if that were only true here. It took me hours. I mean hours to write her name in Japanese on everything. I mean everything. Like, every flashcard in her math kit (there were about 200) and every pencil, eraser, notebook, crayon, colored pencil, tape dispenser, ruler. Everything. Have you ever tried to write your child's name on the side of a plastic penny? I did, and I have a feeling it doesn't look much like "Crescini." The school reasons that they often separate the individual pieces while practicing, so just in case, you should write it on everything.

The paperwork was also endless. Japanese people in general are crazy about paperwork. I think I have spent several months of my life filling out forms in Japan. Of course, all the hassle is worth it because of the great benefits I get from the social welfare system, but it is ridiculously time-consuming. The local ward or city office is the number one tree killer in Japan in my opinion. All the social welfare programs, marriage, death and birth documents, pretty much everything to do with one's identity and residence are run out this single building. There are so many different departments, and none are linked together on one computer system. So when we moved to a new house, we were hopping like bunnies from counter to counter filling out the change of address forms. I have written my address so many times, I think I can write it in Japanese with my eyes closed in my sleep upside down with my toes. You get the picture.

When our kids were born, we spent months filling out paperwork and applying for this and that both on the Japanese side and American side. There is so much paperwork and so many different expiration dates for everything, that we forgot to renew our daughter Abby's residency visa last year. When I had to get a form for a totally unrelated application for something, I noticed that Abby's visa had expired. Of course, since Abby was only three, they were not going to kick her out of the country for her parents' irresponsibility. However, we were required to gather together about 18 different forms to prove we are responsible members of society. We were then summoned to the Regional Immigration Office at Fukuoka Airport (conveniently located in the airport for easy deportation) and after listening to my daughter being addressed several times as *"yogisha,"* which can be translated "suspect," and saying a whole lot of *moshi wake nais* (really sorry for my stupidity), they let Abby the Suspect stay with us for a few more years.

On a more serious note, one of the biggest struggles I have had so far regards the PTA. Unlike in the U.S., PTA committee work is unavoidable in Japan. You can run but you can't hide. At some point during your child's six years in elementary school, you must volunteer (sounds like an oxymoron, doesn't it?). This is an example of the strong Japanese sentiment that everyone must do their part to support each other, children, and society. Being busy is not an excuse. Everyone is busy. You can put it off for a while if you have younger kids at home, or are pregnant, but you cannot avoid it forever.

Not many parents want the extra responsibility of being on the PTA, but are resigned to it, realizing that it is just part of being a parent in Japan. Of course, being a non-native speaker, I could probably lie and say my Japanese is not good enough, but that wouldn't be truthful. Honestly, it does take me much longer to understand stuff, especially written stuff, than a native speaker, but I could probably manage. Being a Christian, as much as I may want to avoid it, I cannot lie and act like language is a hindrance for me. I am now trying to figure out just how hard I want to fight this mandatory volunteerism. Don't misunderstand me, please: I am all for doing my part, but why can't I do my part doing something I am good at, like teaching English at the school or helping translate for all the parents who can't speak Japanese? After all, I have a skill that most parents don't have. I have this sneaking feeling if I do PTA I will have to be the accountant or something crazy like that. I don't think they want me in charge of their money.

I understand that I am going to have a child in the elementary school for the next ten years, so it would be wrong of me to do nothing to support the school that is taking such good care of my kids. But I really take issue in not having control over the timing of when I help or being able to help with something I am strong at. There are several committees, and most parents these days are volunteering for the committee closest to what they might enjoy or be good at to keep from being made to do something they are not good at or don't want to do. I guess I could do this too, but philosophically I have a problem with the PTA system in general.

My blood was boiling recently when I read a letter that Mia brought home about PTA selection for the next academic year. All parents must put their names forward, and then the committee will choose. Since there seems to be a ton of different committees and jobs, the odds of getting selected are probably pretty high. If you are already serving on a committee at another child's school, you are on a neighborhood association, you are currently a PTA member, or you are at home with a small child, you can ask to be left out of the lottery. If you have another good reason for not serving, you have to write the reasons in detail, and then the committee will decide whether that is a good enough reason to be exempted or not. If not, too bad, your name goes into the hat. I can't accept this. My mom, when confronted with something she just outright disagreed with or felt wasn't right would always say, "It's the principal of the thing." That is exactly how I feel.

I thought long and hard before I figured out how to respond to the PTA questionnaire. Finally, I decided that I would try a diplomatic approach first, and see what happens. As much as I dislike the PTA system, there is no need to rock the boat if it is not necessary. I wrote that although I can speak Japanese, reading and writing takes longer for me than for a native speaker. I would appreciate it if they would allow me to serve in another capacity that better suits my skills. I also stated that my husband's Japanese is probably not good enough to serve. Since Emmy is still only three, my friends told me that I probably won't get selected this year anyway. If not, it doesn't really solve my dilemma—it just puts it off for another year. Are they really going to make me serve when my kids are older? Or are they going to think of something else for me to do? I don't know yet. You will have to read my blog to find out!

My Japanese friend also had a problem with all this mandatory volunteerism. She was told she had to make to something for the school bazaar, even though she did not have a sewing machine, or sewing kit, or an ounce of experience or desire to make anything. Couldn't she have volunteered in another way, like baking something or helping out with setup or cleanup? No, she had to make something, which in her case, ended up being cloth lunch bags. So, she called up a friend with a sewing machine and got some needed help in making them. She called this her summer homework assignment. Did she like it? Was she thankful for the experience of learning something new? No, she was miserable and resentful of being made to do something like that and still talks about it today. Of course, being Japanese, she will not be given any slack if she ever decides to rebel and refuse to make lunch bags. Since I'm a foreigner, I might be able to get away with not serving on the PTA, but the environment for Japanese mommies is much harsher and much less forgiving of rebellious behavior.

Ultimately, it all comes down to this: I am very jealous of my time, and I want to decide how I spend it. Spending time with my family is more important to me than anything else. While I gladly will volunteer my time teaching English at the school or baking cookies for a school event, I don't want to spend my time learning to make lunch bags or making copies just because everyone else is doing it. Why does everyone have to do the same thing? Last year Riz and I went to northern Japan to volunteer after the earthquake and tsunami. The most common reaction was, "Wow. That is awesome. I wish I could do that, but I can't." I thought, "Why not? I have three small kids and a full-time job. If I can do it, why can't you?"

Maybe it is hard for Japanese parents, especially mothers, to step outside of their comfort zones. Maybe they think that kind of volunteering is better for people with more freedom: retirees, singles or college students. Most of my friends probably haven't even thought about the possibility of going. I wish sometimes they would think outside the box and channel their amazing volunteering spirits and servant hearts to do some different kinds of volunteering like helping the homeless or volunteering at an orphanage. I am not trying to diminish the value of what they are doing with the PTA or neighborhood association or any other community organization they are volunteering with; I see the value, and their service helps many people. I just want them to expand their concept of what it means to volunteer and serve.

PTA obligations take parents away from children on some weeknights, but recently the school is taking children away more from parents too. Mia's school is gradually implementing Saturday classes, mainly because the Japanese government is bemoaning the decreasing academic ability of today's students. For now, it is just every now and then, but I am sure that eventually it will turn into every Saturday. My husband and I talked about it, and we decided not to send her to school on Saturdays. For us, weekends are family time, a time to relax and be together. The school says Saturday school will be mostly fun stuff and full of activities, but Mia can have fun at home with us.

Maybe you are thinking, "When in Rome, do as the Romans do," and believe me, we have thought a lot about this. For almost everything, we try to fit into Japanese culture and do things the way they do, even if we don't understand it or like it. But when something clashes with our values, our core beliefs, who were are as people, we can't just blindly go along with it. Maybe we are seen as rebels by other parents for not sending her to Saturday school, but that is okay. I don't mind being the nail that sticks out if I am sticking out because of what is best for my family. You can hammer me down all you want. We care more about how our kids see us than how other people see us. We want to do our best to fit into Japanese society, but not at the cost of sacrificing our family time.

We don't know what will happen down the road, but for now, Mia is having a blast in elementary school. She was so excited to go to school the first week that she wanted to put on her shoes and wait in the entranceway, even though she wasn't meeting her friends for another twenty minutes (now we struggle to get her there before they lock they gate). Nine months later, she still loves it, and she has made a lot of good friends. We trust the school with her, and believe they are doing a great job educating her. Of course, it is not perfect for her. Her Japanese is flawless, but her English is much weaker than American kids her age. Her sentences are sometimes unintelligible messes of Japanese and English mixing, and her cultural awareness is suspect. Recently she said, "My English teacher at school is from England, but she still can speak a little English." Yeah, she has a few problems, but how many kids are bilingual at her age?

Our 6-year old, Mia, with her $300 Japanese backpack on her first day of elementary school.

Ideally, there would be a great Christian international school close by with free tuition (I can dream, can't I?), but that is not the case for us. There is no reputable international school nearby, boarding school is not an option, and we have no time for homeschooling. We believe the Japanese education system can provide a great environment for growth for our children in elementary school. However, we do not think the junior high and high school systems are best for our daughters. So, honestly, we have no idea what we are going to do when Mia is ready for junior high. Will we homeschool? Return to the States? We have no idea, but God does, and that is enough for us. Americans I know often hold up the Japanese education system as a model for all to follow, citing higher test scores and the economic success of the Japanese economy. True, Japanese test scores are much higher than ours, and it is hard to argue with that success. But living here, I see the human cost, the lost, stressed-out childhoods and family vacations never taken. There are a lot of things I love and respect about Japan, but the education system is not one of them.

What Does It All Mean?

I first thought of writing this book because I wanted to introduce Japan to people who are new to the country, maybe giving them a heads up about things they didn't know about, things I wish people had told me when I first moved to here. But as I wrote, my intended audience expanded. This book became a book not only for those already living here, but also for those thinking of moving here, or those just interested in the culture. After I finished it, I realized maybe Japanese people would like it, too, learning how people from other cultures may view their own. My dream is to get it translated into Japanese someday soon.

I hope this book offered insights that were helpful and interesting to everyone. I wanted more than anything to present a balanced view of this country, praising what is great, but hopefully causing people to ponder about things that I think are not so great. There are aspects of it that are perfect for me and my family, and others that I think are backwards. There is no perfect place. Generally speaking, people who are dissatisfied with their own countries tend to focus on the good points of their host country, and think it is so wonderful compared to their home country. Conversely, those who love their home countries tend to only see the flaws of their host country. I understand the tendencies towards both ways of thinking, but I think both are unreliable, unrealistic and flawed. The best way to be happy in a new country is to accept the good with the bad, to enjoy the things you love, and accept there are things that you will never understand.

We must always realize that we are guests in our host countries, and if we find ourselves complaining all the time, maybe it is time to go home. However, I have found that people who complain about Japan are general complainers, and they will just find something else to complain about when they go home.

Maybe you are wondering about my family? Well, as of this writing, my husband and I are about to enter our fourteenth year in Japan. What started out as three years turned into five, then into ten and, now, thirteen. Most people who know us just assume that, because we have been here this long, we will never leave. My own mother is one of them. While she sometimes asks when we talk on Skype when we are coming home, I think that deep in her heart she thinks we are here for good. But the truth is, we do not know. Honestly, recently my husband and I have started talking about returning to the States someday. I am feeling restless, longing to do something other than teach English. While I love my job, especially being with the students, there is a stirring in my heart to do something new. My husband wonders if his photography business could be more successful in the U.S. And of course, we are worried about our kids' education. Since we don't want to send them to junior high and high school in Japan, we have five years to think and pray about what the future holds for us.

Ultimately, as Christians, it is not where we want to be, but where God wants us to be. Where will we be most in God's will as a family, doing what He wants us to be doing, being the most useful for His kingdom? I don't know yet the answer to this question. I do know that wherever I live, there has to be Japanese people there. Japan is too much a part of me to ever leave it completely.

So, whether we end up in Japan, the U.S, or somewhere else, Japan will always be in our hearts and in our minds, and we will always be incredibly grateful for the love and hospitality that Japanese people have shown us. Japan is a wonderful, crazy place, and the Japanese people are some of the nicest in the world. If you only remember one thing from this book, I want you to remember that.

Anne Crescini, wife of Riz, mother of Mia, Abby and Emmy, and lover of Japan.

2012

Riz and I celebrating our fourteenth wedding anniversary in 2012.

Share Your Thoughts

Any comments or feedback can be sent to the author at:

anne@drivingmecrazyaboutit.com

For additional book information, and to read Anne's blog posts about life in Japan, please check out the official Driving Me Crazy About It website:

drivingmecrazyaboutit.com

Thanks...

To Jim Xavier, graphic designer/missionary extraordinaire, for the beautiful book cover and website design. You helped make my dream come true in color.

To international award winning photographer Riz Crescini, for providing all the pictures for the book.

To my husband Riz Crescini, for providing unconditional love, unwavering support, and for being my biggest fan.

To Pat and Ron Larson, aka Mom and Dad, for raising me, loving me and always being there for me. And, for giving me a name that is very easy to pronounce in Japanese! I miss you like crazy.

To all the wonderful Japanese people I mentioned in this book, and those I didn't. You are the inspiration for this book.

To my girls Mia, Abby and Emmy. I wouldn't be enjoying this place at all without you, and I would have had nothing to write about. I love being your mommy.

Finally, to God, for loving me and filling my heart with such a great love for my family, and for this country.

4246961R00096

Made in the USA
San Bernardino, CA
07 September 2013